PRAISE FOR *DON'T DITCH THAT TECH*

"*Don't Ditch That Tech* is a rich resource for understanding ways technology can be a thoughtful tool for reaching the complex range of learners in today's classrooms. It is grounded, smart, clever, conversational and practical. The book models differentiation for its readers while it commends differentiation for students. It is likely to become a handbook to which teachers return often rather than a one-and-done read."

—Carol Ann Tomlinson, author, *The Differentiated Classroom*

"Teachers are driven to create personalized experiences for each child, amidst classrooms composed of unique students. That can feel overwhelming. This guide is chock full of tools, apps, graphic images, classroom examples, methods, and practical tips for any classroom educator looking to try new things or further strengthen their current differentiation practices. And it's differentiated for teachers, too!"

**—The HyperDoc Girls (Sarah Landis,
Kelly Hilton, and Lisa Highfill)**

"Matt Miller has done it again! He and Nate and Angelia Ridgway have laid out an easy and successful way to utilize technology in the classroom that puts the emphasis on teaching and learning—and not the device. This is a must have for any teacher or school district trying to implement technology to purposefully impact student learning and growth. This book is full of great examples and ideas and is sure to become the go-to help manual for many teachers. Do yourself a favor and buy this book! You won't be sorry! Warning: Be prepared to see smiling faces on students and engaged classrooms when you do!"

—Holly Clark, author, *The Google Infused Classroom*

"Who knew that *Ditch That Textbook* was the beginning of a trilogy? First: Ditch The Textbook. Then, *Ditch The Homework*. Finally, *Don't Ditch The Tech*. These books have a nice, easy flow that allows educators to easily migrate their pedagogy across the full spectrum of change required to be their best in a modern classroom. This book is the keystone!

"Matt Miller and crew have shared a clear, research-based and meticulous yet fun way for educators to embrace edtech at the highest level. Anecdotes, exemplars and examples abound in this easy to read how-to for any teacher!"

—**Jon Corippo**, Chief Learning Officer, Cue, Inc.

"Interested in marrying your strong teaching practice with transformative tech implementation? Then this book is for you! Written by teachers for teachers, *Don't Ditch The Tech* is brimming with practical advice and guidance to help you take meaningful steps to empower your learners and impact your teaching."

—**Trevor MacKenzie**, coauthor, *Inquiry Mindset,*
and author, *Dive into Inquiry*

"*Don't Ditch That Tech* is full of actionable ideas and resources for educators who want to make the most of classroom technology. With an emphasis on authentic experiences, the authors' passion for digital learning and their practical tips will help every reader reflect and plan strategically this school year!"

—**Monica Burns, EdD,** author, *Tasks Before Apps*

DON'T DITCH THAT TECH

DIFFERENTIATED INSTRUCTION IN A DIGITAL WORLD

MATT MILLER   NATE RIDGWAY   ANGELIA RIDGWAY, PhD

DON'T Ditch That Tech

© 2019 by Matt Miller, Nate Ridgway, and Angelia Ridgway, PhD

This book is available at special discounts when purchased in quantity for use as premiums, promotions, fundraisers, or for educational use. For inquiries and details, contact the publisher at books@daveburgessconsulting.com.

Published by Dave Burgess Consulting, Inc.
San Diego, CA
DaveBurgessConsulting.com

Cover Design by Genesis Kohler
Editing and Interior Design by My Writers' Connection

Library of Congress Control Number: 2019942320
Paperback ISBN: 978-1-949595-50-5
Ebook ISBN: 978-1-949595-48-2
First Printing: June 2019

DEDICATION

To all the educators who think, "There has to be a better way," and do something about it.
—Matt Miller

To Booker, and to all those who will teach him.
—Nate Ridgway

To all my students, including my own family!
—Angie Ridgway

CONTENTS

COPPA AND FERPA NOTICE

Before beginning your journey into the intersection of technology and differentiation, make sure you have studied both COPPA (Children's Online Privacy Protection Act) and FERPA (Family Educational Rights and Privacy Act) guidelines for use with K−12 students and their alignment with your particular school district's policies. The U.S. Department of Education provides suggested language at studentprivacy.ed.gov or check the national guidelines for your home country.

PREFACE

As authors and teachers, we come to the new technological world at very different points in our career. Angie, with the most years in education, started teaching when access to computers was at best limited to home use and the most privileged schools. She acquired tech savviness as a new language which she integrated slowly into her teaching practice. Matt, who is younger, began to integrate instructional technology a few years into his teaching career. Nate, on the other hand, had a not-so-smartphone in hand as a middle schooler and innately integrated technology into the classroom—and every other area of life. As you will see, we've each interacted with technology in different ways throughout our careers in education.

Angie's Long, Long Journey

As the most ancient of this trio, my journey has taken me not only the longest but also the furthest in terms of learning instructional technology. I attribute any natural leanings to my mother, who at almost eighty years young (*shhh!*), grabs every new smartphone and app and uses them like a pro!

I began teaching when teachers would leave the lounge covered in purple mimeo ink. (The great photocopiers were close behind, though.) During student teaching, I lived with a family that had an actual home computer, and I dreamt of the possibilities of using this asset as a Spanish teacher. Fast forward to now, where I have the privilege of preparing future teachers for their careers. I work with the purpose of connecting research and theories to practice. My aim is to prepare my students for the current state of classroom—and for the exciting future that teaching holds. Bring out the crystal ball!

Quite a few theories, authors, and frameworks inform my practice, including Carol Ann Tomlinson (caroltomlinson.com) and Universal Design for Learning (cast.org). Thomas Armstrong and Howard Gardner's research also factor into my thinking and approaches to teacher education (institute4learning.com). You will see references to their tremendous work throughout this book.

So how does a dinosaur like me dip her toe into the tech water? "*Poco a poco*," I would suggest in Spanish. "Little by little." Every semester, I study the latest instructional technologies and thoughtfully add a *few* to my teacher education courses. Otherwise, I can be capricious and overwhelmed. I remind myself that my career was not built in a day and that my tech integration will not be either!

My commitment to myself, my students, and my colleagues is that I choose instructional technologies based on the following principles:

- They are meaningful to learning theory. Don't kick learning science to the curb. Researchers think deeply about how kids learn and have great science that can teach us to be more effective teachers. The integration of technology should not depart from that.

- The learning objective and the standards drive the lesson as do students' needs, not the technology.

- They allow authenticity to flourish in the classroom. As an example, technology has opened the world to language learners. This has revolutionized second-language teaching—and every other content area as well.

- No one has to be a master of every single technology. Today's students are digital natives. Empower them to become experts. But always try the technology before introducing it to your students.

- It's okay to play favorites. I suggest creating a landing spot for your go-to tech tools. I use LiveBinders (livebinders.com) to keep track of mine.

Matt's Road Full of Obstacles

I came to education as a second career. After earning a journalism degree in college, completing several writing internships, and working three months as a professional newspaper reporter, I had learned one thing: I hated the day-to-day beat of covering local news. I also discovered during that time that I loved helping other reporters work through their stories. That was education, not journalism. I went back to college to pursue education and moved into my first classroom in less than a year.

Integrating technology felt like a natural part of my instruction from my first class. I was reared on Commodore and Macintosh, Nintendo and Atari. I used my Palm Pilot extensively in college (and was even scolded by a journalism prof for using it too much lest it fail me in an important moment).

As I look back, one of my earliest memories of classroom tech integration was a telling one. I had installed the CD-ROM of computer activities linked to my Spanish textbooks on a set of laptop computers. I looked across the flickering screens of laptops (attached to external batteries for extra life!), crossed my arms, and smiled. *Look at this*, I thought. *Where's my principal? Where's my camera? This has to be what true twenty-first-century teaching looks like.*

It didn't take long for me to start rethinking my satisfaction. What if these programs are no different than handing my students workbooks and worksheets? I wondered. Are my students actually learning better—and more?

Even as I noticed the faults in my early tech integration, I could see the potential of those devices. I saw the future! Well before powerful tablets, smartphones, and Chromebooks came on the scene, I *knew* that technology, when used properly as a teaching tool, could help our students learn more efficiently and effectively—and in a way that uniquely fit who they were.

Nate's Latest Experience:
Flipping a Classroom

In my fourth year of teaching, one of my department heads at my high school noticed that I had an unusually high number of students in my dual credit U.S. History course. She noticed how much I already used technology in my classroom—interactive Google Slides, other web-based apps, etc.—and suggested that I consider flipping my classroom. This would allow students to attend in person or online—a choice of differentiation that could allow me to better meet my students' needs. To be honest, I had never considered flipping my classroom and had very little idea of what it would take.

Now, a few months later, I've realized how much work goes into designing a course like this. I've had to push my digital skills in ways I hadn't expected:

- I've learned to design interactive, online tutorials for students.

- I've uploaded my consciousness to the internet in the form of YouTube videos and learned how to live stream. (You can see my efforts here: youtube.com/ridgwayhistory.)

- And most importantly, I've learned to push the limits of differentiation through technology.

In a way, the flipping skills that I had to learn trace back to the goal that Matt, Angie, and I have for this book: to give you a developmental toolkit of tech differentiation of your own. Don't worry if acquiring these skills takes time. Everyone, me included, started as a beginner at one point.

WHAT IS DIFFERENTIATION ANYWAY?

> The idea of differentiating instruction is an approach to teaching that advocates active planning for and attention to student differences in classrooms, in the context of high-quality curriculums.
>
> —CAROL ANN TOMLINSON

Differentiation means meeting students where they are not only developmentally but also based on their interests, culture, knowledge, experiential base, and attention—which can vary by the moment! As we explore the ways technology allows for differentiated learning, you will see our ideas of technological integration anchored in phrases, such as anticipating learning, grabbing attention, accessing content, transparency, personalization, processes, culture, authenticity, and product. Some of these phrases might sound familiar because they emanate from well-known educational thinkers, writers, and scholars. These concepts help us all develop practical ways to meet varied learners' needs with the support of technology.

We hope that the suggestions in this book can help you be better at differentiation, no matter your entry point.

And why the partnership between differentiation and technology? At its very core, technology is a tool. From the beginning of human history, people have designed tools to make life more efficient. Education technology, especially in the past few decades, has become like an ever-expanding Swiss Army Knife. We have access to a wealth of different and powerful tools to help us meet our students' unique needs. Universal Design for Learning (UDL, cast.org) is the best advocate for opening up students' varied access to learning.

Here are just a few ways differentiating through tech can improve your teaching practice:

- Create and maintain highly engaging learning experiences.

- Deliver meaningful, truly authentic instruction.

- Meet more students' specific needs and engage their interests (to the point that they'll think, "Wow, this class was *made* for me!").

- Transform your classroom into a student-centered environment by empowering your learners to do the heavy lifting intellectually and academically.

- Help students understand how they think, so they better know how to learn (metacognition).

- Make teaching easier and more *fun*!

WHAT CAN YOU DO WITH TECHNOLOGY?

Like any tool in a teacher's kit, technology possesses strengths, limitations, and purpose in the context of a learning environment and a well-designed lesson. So before we get into specific ways to use technology in your classroom, let's look at what it *cannot* do:

Technology cannot be:

- done for the sake of itself; it is *not* the learning goal.

- implemented without layers of support and differentiation; hey, that's this book!

- executed without training or preparation by students and staff.

- a learning panacea-a cure-all for poor teaching and struggling teachers.

What *can* it do? Technology can supercharge learning. It can help pique the interest of the most reluctant learner. Technology can help us as teachers craft a learning environment that fits our students like a glove.

The TPACK Model anchors many of these tenets. The integration of instructional technology should be a meaningful blend of technological, pedagogical, and content-based (knowledge) approaches. TPACK is like a three-legged stool. When technology, pedagogy, or content are deployed poorly, the stool is imbalanced and suffers. When we strengthen our practice in any area, we make the stool sturdy enough to support our weight. More in-depth study of this approach can be found at tpack.org.

In short, technology can amplify our best teacher features *and* free us up to do what we're uniquely, wonderfully created to do:

build relationships with our students, help them when they struggle, and encourage them to reach new heights. That's at the heart of the five main principles of this book.

THE FIVE PRINCIPLES OF DON'T DITCH THAT TECH

1. Technology should be used to enhance students' learning and should rely on evidence-based practices. There is *no* substitute for great teaching or great student-to-teacher relationships.

2. Technology should help us work with content in interactive, meaningful ways.

3. Technology should help teachers and students cross varied developmental levels.

4. Technology should eventually empower students to be designers of their own learning. The goal is for students to become critical thinkers and life-long learners.

5. Technology should promote reflection and metacognition.

As you journey through these next chapters, the above five principles will serve as your foundation of great teaching and sound instructional design. In the following chapters, you will receive countless, practical, tangible examples of how to implement new ideas in class and fine-tune your tech skills to meet the ever-changing and varied needs of your students. Here is a brief overview of what is in store with chapters labeled with letters that spell "DITCH IT!" as a nod to our title:

- **Chapters D** and **I** start your journey by helping you analyze your current level of differentiation with technology. We'll discuss a few apps here, but we'll mostly explore your current level of teaching practice and what's possible with the resources around you. It is *differentiated for you.*

- **Chapters T, C, H,** and **I** examine how to manipulate tech to differentiate it for the purposes of lesson design. The key terms highlighted in these chapters are *attention, personalization, choice, authenticity, process, product,* and others that support differentiation.

- The final two chapters, **T** and **!,** extend tech and differentiation beyond your lesson to start considering how to be more *transparent* in your teaching (especially with students and families in mind) and how to employ technology to develop *metacognitive practices.*

Let's do it!

—Nate, Angie, and Matt

DOING WHAT I DO, DIGITALLY

T echnology has been enhancing learning since the Stone Age. Technically, the first tablets (stone ones) served as a way to improve people's ability to preserve and document knowledge. They were slightly more durable than iPads but much less versatile! While the tablet phenomenon has certainly undergone a few revolutions since its earliest days, our desire to find more efficient and effective ways to learn has not.

We all enter the tech integration process at different points and with diverse talents and needs. (Remember the widely varying backgrounds the three of us shared in the preface.) Our students have diverse talents and needs, too, but for now, let's just focus on you, the teacher.

Don't you love a survey? Think of this one like one of those fun personality profiles people share on Facebook—only way more practical! Your answers will help you find where you can best level up your tech game in the classroom.

You can also take the survey online:
dontditchtech.com/survey

1. I tend to lead the use of technology in the classroom.

	1	2	3	4	
Agree	☐	☐	☐	☐	Disagree

2. Students provide limited input on my content/curriculum.

	1	2	3	4	
Agree	☐	☐	☐	☐	Disagree

3. I create opportunities for students to interact with my classroom content.

	1	2	3	4	
Disagree	☐	☐	☐	☐	Agree

4. Students are generally given many choices in terms of interaction with me and their classmates via technology.

	1	2	3	4	
Disagree	☐	☐	☐	☐	Agree

5. I provide students with varied options to learn new content.

	1	2	3	4	
Disagree	☐	☐	☐	☐	Agree

6. Students can make choices in my classroom from a list of interactive technologies.

	1	2	3	4	
Disagree	☐	☐	☐	☐	Agree

7. I modify my content/curriculum based upon student input within the boundaries of my standards.

	1	2	3	4	
Disagree	☐	☐	☐	☐	Agree

8. What I teach each day has already been decided before my students enter the room.

	1	2	3	4	
Agree	☐	☐	☐	☐	Disagree

9. Students' input and needs drive the content and skills I teach each year in my classroom.

	1	2	3	4	
Disagree	☐	☐	☐	☐	Agree

10. My students receive specific, quality feedback that helps them think about how they think and learn (metacognition).

	1	2	3	4	
Disagree	☐	☐	☐	☐	Agree

Now, go ahead and total your score: _____

WHAT DOES MY SCORE MEAN?

 If you scored from 0–16, you are a **Pilot**.

Look for the pilot's hat icon in the text to read more about yourself.

 If you scored from 17–22, you are a **Museum Exhibitor.**

Look for the vase icon in the text to read more about yourself.

 If you scored from 23–28, you are a **Restaurant Owner**.

Look for the flatware icon in the text to read more about yourself.

 If you scored from 29–34, you are a **Councilmember.**

Look for the meeting icon in the text to read more about yourself.

 If you scored from 35-40, you are a **Creative Art Coach.**

Look for the idea icon in the text to read more about yourself.

These five roles correspond to different levels of a continuum of technology integration and differentiation. (See the chart below.) Remember, these roles are not static; you aren't defined by your role forever! Nor do these roles define a *good* or a bad *teacher*. Rather they give us a starting point for self-analysis and improved, differentiated, instructional practice.

As you reflect on your role, you might well discover that it varies based on the project at hand. For example, you might rate yourself as a Restaurant Owner for anticipatory sets but see yourself as a Pilot for creating student projects. Never fear! This book is differentiated for you too.

Let's check them out!

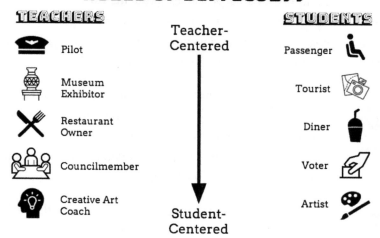

TECH DIFFERENTIATION: ROLES OF DIFFICULTY

TEACHERS		STUDENTS
Pilot	Teacher-Centered	Passenger
Museum Exhibitor		Tourist
Restaurant Owner		Diner
Councilmember		Voter
Creative Art Coach	Student-Centered	Artist

In the **Pilot's** classroom, the teacher has almost total control over his or her passengers' content, process, and interaction. Pilots differentiate based on their own choices and preferences. Just like in an airplane, students are along for the ride and can't change the course of their journey. Examples of tech utilized by a Pilot might include PowerPoint presentations, 1:1 note-taking, and online textbooks.

 A **Museum Exhibitor's** classroom features a new level of tech differentiation: *interactivity*. Like any modern-day museums, however, all students still experience the same processes and content because they experience the same exhibits. Apps used by the Museum Exhibitor might include group-led Kahoot! games, Plickers, and other one-size-fits-all strategies.

 A **Restaurant Owner's** room is more differentiated than either the Pilot or the Museum Exhibitor. Students are given interactive choices on how to learn. The meal (the content) is the same, but students choose from a menu of learning processes. Students do not have high levels of input on the content or curriculum. Examples of technology integration in this classroom could include traditional PowerPoint/Google Slides presentations, Prezi, and Canva.

 A **Councilmember's** classroom includes *some student input on the content under study.* The elements of interactive technology and choice remain. An example of tech integration in this classroom might include using the app Socrative to gather student feedback to change lesson content.

 A **Creative Art Coach's** classroom is truly the definition of a student-centered, differentiated environment. It features decision-making input from all parties as well as high-quality, specific feedback from a teacher who acts like a coach. In this classroom, you'll see student-led research projects using a variety of technologies to facilitate varied content, processes, and expressions of knowledge.

SO WHAT'S NEW AT EACH LEVEL?

TEACHERS			STUDENTS
	Pilot	Teacher-Led Technology	Passenger
	Museum Exhibitor	Interactive Tech	Tourist
	Restaurant Owner	Student-Chosen Process	Diner
	Councilmember	Student-Chosen Content	Voter
	Creative Art Coach	Student-Driven Content & Quality Feedback	Artist

How to Get Started

Like any kind of change, altering your approach to technological differentiation in your classroom should be taken step by step. No one teacher can alter his or her pedagogy on a dime; instead, small praxis-based (reflection, practice, repeat) efforts should enable your continued development. Take it *poco a poco*, little by little. As you know, it takes time for you and your students to build the skills, proficiencies, and interests necessary for any kind of success. Tech works the same way.

What follows is a framework created with the goal of meeting your developmental needs as you strive to help your individual students succeed. As such, it will guide you through growing from a Pilot to a Creative Art Coach or somewhere in between. After all, we are differentiating for you too!

You've got this! Onward!

1

IDENTIFYING YOUR TECH SITUATION AND EXPLORING POSSIBILITIES

PART 1:
WHEN CLASSROOM TECH GOES B.A.D.

In this era of increasing instructional technology in schools, we hear common questions repeated:

1. How can I use technology in my classroom if my school hasn't provided it?

2. How do I differentiate for my students based on what I have on hand?

With those questions in mind, this chapter is differentiated for you, a teacher in a particular place, at a particular point in your development, with particular access to tech. The ultimate goal is to equip you to best meet the varied student needs in your classroom.

As you move through this Parts 1 and 2 of this chapter, we encourage you to do the following:

1. Identify your current level of access to technology in the classroom.

2. Analyze how this affects your ability to differentiate.

3. Explore solutions that will allow you to employ technology to differentiate within your circumstances.

We want to acknowledge that even though technology has increasingly become part of the classroom environment, not every teacher has the ability to have a student on a device at all times. But limited access to iPad/Chomebook carts, computer labs, and even student smartphones doesn't mean limited ways to differentiate with tech. We have the opportunity to harness the power of all technology in our classrooms—whether school-issued or not—in ways that can transform students' learning. When we make these devices that students bring to school part of our plan, we call it a B.A.D. (Bring A Device) environment. (To be clear, we're not saying technology is *bad*. We're saying B.A.D. can be wonderful!)

Let's classify the two general and different scenarios that most teachers find themselves in with regards to available technology:

B.A.D. (Smartphone or 1:1, see below)	Teacher and students are equipped with a personal device, either their own or a school-provided one.
Cart/Lab	Students have access to a computer cart or a computer lab.

When we preview how the tech-access scenarios (above) would look in a few different classrooms, each with different technology available to them, you'll notice a couple of common threads:

1. The teachers we show off below *tailor* their use of technology to their lesson objectives, not vice-versa. Again the theme of "technology is a tool, not a lesson plan" should sound familiar.

2. These teachers attempt to *tie up any loose ends* by critically thinking about their use of tech in the classroom. They try to be *proactive problem-expecters* instead of *reactive problem-solvers*.

B.A.D. (mostly Smartphones)	B.A.D. (1 to 1 with tablet or laptop)	Cart/Lab Set-Up
Mr. Jamie's Tenth-Grade History Classroom	Ms. Arowen's Sixth-Grade Science Classroom	Miss Wilson's Fourth-Grade Classroom
Lesson Topic: The Inca Empire	**Lesson Topic:** Kinetic and Potential Energy	**Lesson Topic:** Two-Digit Multiplication
Major Concerns: Device Access and Expectations	**Major Concerns:** Standardized Devices and Expectations	**Major Concerns:** Consistent Availability and Resource Distribution
Tailoring the Tech I really want my students to visualize the architectural achievements of the Inca Empire, so I'll use a few Wi-Fi-enabled cell-phones that were donated to the class as a virtual tour guide. *Here's my example:* dontditchtech.com/tailor1	**Tailoring the Tech** My school's 1:1 Chromebooks allow students to create simulated models and reflect on their learning. *Here's my example:* dontditchtech.com/tailor2	**Tailoring the Tech** A Cart/Lab will allow me to provide students with lots of example problems that they can try and then evaluate with their peers. *Here's my example:* dontditchtech.com/tailor3

Tying Up Loose Ends	Tying Up Loose Ends	Tying Up Loose Ends
I'll need to be careful to make sure all students can access a smartphone in class and to prevent stigma against those who do not own a device. I should also remind students of our smartphone use policy after their warm-up activity.	Two of my students don't consistently keep their Chromebooks charged; I'll need to keep a couple of chargers on hand to make sure they can participate. I'll also review Chromebook expectations before the lesson starts so that it goes smoothly.	Because my students aren't in the computer lab each day, my lesson will have to be confined to a single-day activity or be completed at home. If the lab isn't available today, I can get access to a cart of iPads and use a HyperDoc, so students can quickly access the day's resources.

The rest of this chapter is dedicated to exploring these two arrangements, B.A.D. and Cart/Lab, in depth. Before we begin: You might be tempted to skip past a section that doesn't exactly describe your technology arrangement. That's up to you. But consider resisting that temptation! Technology use in each section will likely still work in yours too. For instance, 360° YouTube videos, which work in B.A.D. smartphone-based classrooms, are highly useful for a 1:1 teacher as well.

- And don't forget! The following sections below, just like the previous chapters, will be targeted to your current skill level (Pilot, Museum Exhibitor, Restaurant Owner, Councilmember, Creative Art Coach) with technology as well.

B.A.D. (Bring a Device) itself can be further divided into two separate categories, smartphones and other devices, though we generally approach how we teach them similarly. See the chart below.

WHEN TECH GOES B.A.D.

SMARTPHONES
Students use a
personal cellular
device, such as an
iPhone or Android

):1
Students use a device,
such as a Chromebook
or tablet, provided by
the school

Of the two, differentiating with smartphones is particularly challenging. Let's look at how to make it work.

THE FIRST HALF OF B.A.D.: SMARTPHONES

Although many teachers see smartphones as just another distraction, these devices can be powerful in the classroom. Smartphones are tactile, highly visual, and provide access to expertly developed apps. Plus, because they are *mobile*, these devices let students take learning and creating wherever they go—in the classroom or in the world. If you ban smartphones in class entirely, you might accidentally eliminate the best devices available for learning. We know from experience that smartphones can spark learning in your students' hands more than a shoe organizer on your classroom door.

In many classrooms, *one teacher* has access to a device (e.g., a laptop connected to a projector), and *some students* have access to a smartphone. If this sounds like your own room, you're probably already aware that *access* and *appropriate use* are the main problems you face.

Let's discuss access first. According to The Pew Research Center in its 2018 report, 95 percent of teens have a smartphone or access to one. Although this statistic makes it sound like smartphones are ubiquitous, remember that possession is just one component of access. We must account for internet access and consistent functionality too.

A good way to implement a B.A.D. experience in your classroom is to have your students take a survey at the beginning of the year. Having parents/guardians take part, too, helps to ensure that everyone's on the same page with the answers. We suggest asking the following questions:

- Who has unlimited data?
- Who has enough data and is willing to use some in class?
- Would you be willing to share your phone with others in class?
- Does your family have any old smartphones (and their chargers) to donate to our class?

Note: You can still use smartphones with no data if they use apps that don't require the internet or if you can connect with them to school wi-fi.

The data you gather with a survey can help you plan instruction and find solutions for stigma around smartphone access.

And a note about stigma: Because not all students have the same access to personal technology, addressing stigma is an especially important next step if you plan to do B.A.D. Five percent of students in a class of thirty means that on average, rounding upwards, two of your students will not have a smartphone. Depending on your class size and student demographics, these numbers could be lower or very well much higher.

MATT'S ADVICE

Need more devices in your classroom? Do a smartphone drive with families. Once they're updated and include a charge cord, any student can make use of them with the help of your school's wi-fi (if available).

Be prepared to have the difficult but honest conversation about access to smartphones. This conversation can go a long way in creating a safe, socially inclusive, digital, work environment. The last thing you want to do when integrating technology is to make a student feel he or she is a lesser human being because he or she doesn't have a smartphone. That student is probably already dealing with that feeling and might confront it daily. Reopening that wound can have very negative consequences.

How this conversation goes exactly is up to you, but we recommend sticking to this key idea: Not owning a smartphone is perfectly fine because most activities in class will not require one, but when we do need to use them, we are a learning community that will ensure all members can participate.

GROUPING AND PROCEDURES/EXPECTATIONS

Choosing to use smartphones or other collected devices in your class will require you to thoughtfully create your groupings, expectations, and procedures accordingly and adapt your lessons to your students' digital access. Don't have a device for each student? Let's talk about *grouping*.

IDEAS FOR SMALL GROUPS, EACH WITH ONE DEVICE

- Allow students to sketch ideas first on large poster paper that your class eventually turns into a digital creation that represents their collective thinking (using your own device). The advantages of this are that you only need to set up one device, and as groups share their paper-based sketches, students get to hear others' thinking and organization.

- Assign specific group roles (limit groups to no more than four members) and have each group design a chart or slide on that group's preferred application. Or have each group review a portion of a resource like a digital textbook and share it via a jigsaw exercise. Again, these strategies feature the benefit of group processing, but you only need to learn a few apps and require only few devices in the classroom at once.

IDEAS FOR A TECH STATION

If you have three or four class smartphones or devices, create a station-based activity set where one table can hold the devices for all students. Some apps really mesh nicely with this setup. Here are a few of our favorites:

- **Padlet (padlet.com):** Create a board where students can respond.

- **Flipgrid (flipgrid.com):** Students use short video responses to interact with and share content.

- **Answer Garden (answergarden.ch):** Students respond to a question with a word or short phrase.

- **BackChannelChat (backchannelchat.com):** Students interact in a chatroom-style discussion board.

PRACTICAL SMALL GROUP OR STATION-BASED APPS

We shared three of our favorites, but there are so many options to consider. Here's a more comprehensive list of apps to make use of in small groups or stations.

App	Link
Classtime	classtime.com
BackChannelChat	backchannelchat.com
Quizizz	quizizz.com
Google Forms	google.com/forms
Kahoot	create.kahoot.it
Flipgrid	flipgrid.com
AnswerGarden	answergarden.ch
Padlet	padlet.com

EXPECTATIONS AND PROCEDURES

Apps aside, the expectations and procedures that will need to be addressed in a B.A.D. classroom are arguably more important:

- When should smartphones or small devices be used?

- How will your class put them away/take them out? What procedures are part of these scenarios? How will you cue students? (Don't forget to practice and remind them!)

- What do you do when students forget the smartphone or their battery is dead?

- How will students share smartphones with their peers?

Nate's own basic digital expectations and procedures in his classroom look something like this:

MR. RIDGWAY'S RULES AND EXPECTATIONS

- Smartphones are an academic, not social, tool in my classroom.

- I will let you (the students) know the appropriate time to use your cellular device. If we're not using them, put them in your backpack, purse, etc.

- If you have a table partner without a smartphone, share your device with him or her.

- Headphones cannot be used while we're using smartphones in class.

You might be tempted to go into extreme depth with rules, processes, and regulations, but don't forget the most important part of your classroom management plan: a well-designed, engaging lesson. Students in Nate's class often comment or complain that: "We're too busy to get on our phones." Engaging and dynamic lessons can solve a lot of cell-phone related problems before they even start.

> THE MOST IMPORTANT PART OF YOUR
> CLASSROOM MANAGEMENT PLAN: A
> WELL-DESIGNED, ENGAGING LESSON.

THE OTHER HALF OF B.A.D.: 1:1

If your students are showing up to your classroom with their own devices in hand or one that the school has provided them, you're in luck, access-wise. Your students are more consistently connected than in a smartphone or Cart/Lab scenario, which initially puts you on better footing.

A TIP FROM NATE

Because students' cell phones are their own, carefully monitor their use of devices. They can easily become distracted while you might struggle to monitor what their screen is on! Make sure you set clear expectations with your students and circulate around the room frequently.

Your Device's Strengths and Weaknesses

If your school is 1:1, the decision on which device students will use likely has already been made. Each device has its own strengths:

- **iPads** are for creating images and video. They're also very tactile and intuitive, which lends itself to the youngest learners who can't read or type yet. The lack of a physical keyboard on iPads makes typing a chore (even with an external keyboard connected). The number of apps that are preloaded and expected to be used is often a school or departmental decision.

- **Chromebooks** are lightning fast, especially when they start up. They're built for the web, so they excel when students do work in web browsers. The downside is that you can't install some software on them, such as Microsoft Word.

- **Windows laptops** are versatile. You can install software on them and work efficiently in a web browser. They can be big and bulky, however, and tend to slow down a lot over time.

- **MacBooks** are powerful. They're the industry standard for video production, design, and creative work. They adeptly handle the massive programs you need for video, design, and image editing. Their significant "weakness" is cost; they can be expensive, and students can be rough on devices.

When a school or district adopts a certain type of device across the board, it locks everyone into a set of strengths and weaknesses. If you have a chance before decisions are made, advocate for what you think is best for your school or district. (Contrary to popular belief, the decision doesn't have to be one certain device for every student and every classroom. Giving students device choices can be a great idea too!)

If that decision has already been made, get to know the strengths and weaknesses of the devices you have. This can help you plan your lessons accordingly and improve your chances of success. For example, let's say you want students to reflect on a reading and share their opinions and thoughts. If they have Chromebooks or a laptop, you might opt to use a quick assignment in Formative (goformative.com) or a short answer in Socrative (socrative.com). If they have iPads, you might choose a video response with a tool like Flipgrid (flipgrid.com). Could you do a text-based Formative or Socrative assignment on an iPad? Could you do a Flipgrid response with a laptop or Chromebook? Definitely *yes* to both! You might give preference to one over the other, however, because of speed or ease of use on the devices you have available. You and your students will find your preferences as you practice and become comfortable with your devices.

ANGIE'S RECOMMENDATION

Develop a mechanism for sampling different apps across different devices. On your own, try various apps with any device you might have lying around: a MacBook laptop, iPad, or a computer lab PC. If you need more testing, a student helper or tech-savvy colleague can help you do further tests for variation. App wise, Microsoft or Google login-enabled apps are an extra valuable find because your students (assuming they have a Microsoft or Google account) are nearly guaranteed an easy login for use across multiple devices.

THE LIMITATIONS OF 1:1

The limitations of 1:1 generally revolve around consistency issues. If your school has students bring their own devices (BYOD), teachers must be aware that varied devices can cause inconsistent access and the inability to see student screens. Even if your school does provide a common device, such as iPads or Chromebooks, be prepared for occasional issues, including leaving devices at home, forgetting to charge devices, or broken-down devices. Angie keeps an old iPad in her teaching cart for just such occasions.

No matter how students get their device, though, 1:1 demands that teachers develop numerous policies (both schoolwide and classroom-specific), such as appropriate use in the learning environment, the need to charge in class, and rules on missing devices. Most of these decisions will be based on a combination of personal preferences and experiences and the expectations of school administrators.

Consider your choices carefully, though. In Nate's classroom, for instance, he frequently has students use their school-provided 1:1 devices, so he lets students charge their Chromebooks as needed, a choice that requires seating modifications on the fly to make that possible. Nate's solution for the 2018–2019 school year was to implement flexible seating so that his students could move and sit around the class as needed. Three desks in the back of the room are designated as recharging stations.

Any decision with 1:1 use in the classroom will likely have consequences that extend further than expected. Remain flexible and find solutions that work best for you and your students.

PLANNING AND ADAPTING YOUR LESSONS WITH B.A.D.

Assuming that you are willing to take up the challenge, how can you do B.A.D. well and differentiate it? (Remember again that B.A.D. means "Bring A Device." The irony that we just said "do B.A.D. well" isn't lost on us, and more of those funny moments are coming!) Let's take a look.

B.A.D. Pilots

If you're a Bring a Device Pilot with a load of passengers and don't have a computer cart or lab available, don't worry! You can still do so much to integrate tech and differentiate learning. The list below might give you a few places to start. Remember *poco a poco*.

24

ANTICIPATORY SETS AND ASSESSMENTS

Start your lesson well with a question, probe, or video that sparks student interest.

> **Note:** Regardless of the number of devices in the room, you can embed multiple levels of critical thinking.

PLICKERS

Looking for a way to do a quick warm up? Try Plickers (plickers.com). After prompting the whole class with one or more questions, students raise a QR-code-looking piece of paper (rotated a certain way to show A, B, C, or D), and you scan the room with your smartphone. Plickers will display all the students' responses in a neat, tidy, summary screen. Students don't need a device to use this app, so it's especially convenient for elementary or cell-phone-free classrooms. Why not differentiate the questions based on levels of thinking? Posing varied questions and analyzing results will allow you to deepen student learning and to challenge those who excel.

ANGIE'S ADVICE

As with any technology or teaching technique, you generally might wait to attempt a program like Plickers after several sessions of modeling and practice. Gradually build it into your teaching repertoire. Sometimes it's best to use a new app with old content so that students don't have two new experiences at once!

Require all students to answer key questions and to choose from questions that push their thinking. The additional questions can be linked to varied levels of Bloom's Taxonomy or Webb's Depth of Knowledge (DOK). If, for example, the concept was plant growth and reproduction from third-grade science, you could create codes that answered different questions from varied levels of Bloom's Taxonomy and Webb's Depth of Knowledge (dontditchtech.com/blooms):

1. List the items a plant needs to grow (answers in groups of two or three).

2. What happens if a plant does not have enough water? (varied answers as multiple choice).

3. Given a live plant, predict what part might help with plant reproduction; label the plant to correspond to the multiple-choice answers. (This question involves more formal thinking.)

Apps for the Rest of Your Lesson

Once you have students hooked, how can you use tech to vary the balance of your lessons? Why not try the following?

Matt's Thoughts on Thinking Ahead

Once you have the videos you want to use, think about how your students can access them:

- Create a class website so that students can access videos any time even away from school.

- If you have your own videos that you would like students to see, add them to Google Drive. You can provide a link to access them.

YouTube (youtube.com)

You can find videos suitable for any area of content on YouTube. With a projector and some speakers, one well-placed YouTube video could:

- make a tricky idea more visible and understandable,

- provide a visual for a model or an item (like a large animal) that can't be in the classroom, helping incorporate varied background knowledge and experience,

- help students learn how to do certain skill through a tutorial, or

- engage students at the outset of your lesson or provide a capstone for a larger unit objective.

Consider Angie's Arenas on page 79 as a starting point for where to find quality content. Many educational channels also provide links to channels that cover similar content areas, and you can generally find recommendations on your homepage that are more suited to your individual classroom, teaching style, or your students' interests.

Read More: "10 Ways YouTube Can Engage Your Classes Now" DitchThatTextbook.com/youtubeengage

Wheel Decide (wheeldecide.com)

Finally, let's include a couple of apps that will make your life easier. "Wheel Decide" is an online random item selector. You can customize the labels with student names, questions for students to answer, themes to study, or anything you'd like. It's a way to have some intentionality in your differentiation. Nate has used a wheel with numbers one through fifty on it, paired with a series of study strategies that differentiate based off students' preferences—just imagine! Check out the wheel here (dontditchtech.com/wheel) and the accompanying Google Doc here (dontditchtech.com/wheeldoc).

GRADECAM (GRADECAM.COM)

If you need to grade lots of student tests and quizzes or create a few different (leveled) versions *based on student need,* use GradeCam. Similar to how Plickers takes student data and scans it with your smartphone, GradeCam does the same with a Scantron-looking form that students complete. You can also transfer the grades to most electronic gradebooks, analyze class data, and use the information for *intentional lesson design and grouping.*

OTHER B.A.D. PILOT OPTIONS

- **Ditty (dontditchtech.com/ditty):** expresses your texts in a song and one device is all that is needed to create and show students

- **BuniComic (bunicomic.com):** blank comics for use at different levels that employ student input and use one created comic for all to enjoy

- **Aww App (awwapp.com):** turns your device into a whiteboard for small group or class teaching

Read More: "10 ways to collaborate digitally + visually in class with Aww App" DitchThatTextbook.com/awwapp

- **ClassDojo (classdojo.com):** behavior management and online classroom community for K–6 classrooms

Remember, these pilot-level ideas are just a starting point. As you become more comfortable (and you and your students level up your tech skills), continue to look for ways that tech can help students learn more efficiently and effectively. When we use technology to do what we always have done with the paper, we squander its true potential!

B.A.D. MUSEUM EXHIBITOR

Tech integration increases with each new level along the continuum. The Museum Exhibitor uses the most accessible tech—a smartphone—to promote *interactivity* at a level beyond that of the Pilot. Don't be fooled by the size of a device. Even if your tech is somewhat limited, the interaction, combined with the fact that students are inclined to be on their phones, makes it easy to bump up engagement!

ANTICIPATORY SETS AND ASSESSMENTS

GOOGLE FORMS (FORMS.GOOGLE.COM)

Google's version of a survey or assessment is easy to use on mobile devices and can provide you some solid ways to analyze formative and summarize data. Customization abounds here with options like making the form a quiz, which can assign point values to questions or select which questions appear in the form based on student performance.

> **Read More:** "Twenty Practical Ways to Use Google Forms in Class/School" DitchThatTextbook.com/googleforms

NATE'S TIPS

Google Forms provides many easily customizable templates for you to use. Start with one of these. You can learn to create your own forms once you become more familiar with how the app works.

Just like any Google Document or Slide, Google Forms are shareable, and the data from them can be downloaded on to a Google Sheet for further analysis. *Nice*!

QUIZIZZ AND KAHOOT! (QUIZIZZ.COM AND KAHOOT.COM)

Assessment is fun and easy with Kahoot! Quizizz. Quizizz is a great Kahoot! alternative that adds student-paced questions, funny memes, and lots of extra features that make it a useful, interactive, and fun tool. And just like Kahoot!, it features a library full of questions that you can pull from to make your own quizzes. Students love the competitive element, and it looks great on mobile. Kahoot!'s graphics and shape-represented answers appeal to younger students, but both applications can be used to analyze student data and reteach content.

Make the most of the interaction with these apps by being sure you close the loop after using them! Use students' captivated attention as a conduit to conduct some re-teaching and promote reflection (See Chapter !) from the data you have gathered. After answering a Kahoot! question, students are still mentally engaged with that question. Their minds are receptive to feedback and additional examples. Don't miss that opportunity!

> ***Read More:*** "Using Kahoot! and Others the Way Your Brain Craves" DitchThatTextbook.com/kahootbrain

AnswerGarden (answergarden.ch)

Great for quick warm ups and exit tickets, AnswerGarden creates word clouds based on submissions from your students. It's a fun way to incorporate their varied cultures and lived experiences. Just remember to set clear expectations for how or what your students post and to make your prompts clear.

Nate's Tip

When you send a link to your students to use AnswerGarden, the normal link will send students to a page where they can see their peers' answers. If you want them to submit an idea without being influenced by others, do the following:

- Take a normal link like: answergarden.ch/616021
- Add in an "**m/**" before the numbers: answergarden.ch/m/616021

You can project the whole-class results using the original link once all students have submitted their ideas.

Backchannel Chat (backchannelchat.com)

Apps like Backchannel Chat allow a teacher with limited devices to use content or content questions for student-driven input and processing. These backchannels prompt digital natives to use "social media-like" forums to process content and make meaningful connections to engage the long-term memory.

ANGIE'S EXAMPLE

While teaching her course on "Culture and Climate of Schools," Angie created a Backchannel Chat for teacher candidates to discuss a prompt related to an article they had read. Apps like this one were used intentionally because they work well on student phones and create a transcript for the teacher to analyze learning outcomes.

INTERACTIVE TECH FOR OTHER PARTS OF YOUR LESSON

360° CITIES

This online site can provide 3-D virtual tours of sites from around the globe—highly useful for foreign language, geography, or history courses, or even as writing prompts or background knowledge for literature. What makes 360° especially dynamic is that it syncs with most phones' gyroscopes, which means that the virtual camera in Singapore, for instance, turns wherever the user looks.

ANGIE'S ADVICE

Speaking of 360° cities, did you know that some YouTube videos are 360° as well? These can provide an incredibly immersive experience for students with their own devices. You have to experience one to see what we mean. Try these out:

- Race in Roman Chariot: dontditchtech.com/chariot
- Running of the Bulls in Pamplona: dontditchtech.com/bulls

Deepen learning by combining virtual reality (VR) with a variety (differentiated levels) of prompts and questions. Have students write about or discuss these locales. Here's an example from a reflection piece used after a VR experience on the battlefield at Gettysburg. Notice how the increase in higher-level thinking proceeds:

- Describe the land (terrain) around Gettysburg.

- What advantages or disadvantages might this have caused for Union and Confederate forces?

- Compare the three different sources: The VR of 360° Cities experience of Little Round Top, the terrain map, and the army positioning map. If you were a Union or Confederate general, where would your primary concern be? And why?

SKYPE AND GOOGLE HANGOUTS

Face-to-face meeting apps can provide students with an authentic means of exploring the world. These tools should also be recognized for their interactive ability to connect individuals or a whole classroom, depending on your school or classroom procedures. Skype, Google Hangouts, and Zoom (where available) can bring the world to your classroom. Consider these uses:

- Invite guest speakers for career talks, even at varied stations for a team of elementary students.

- Recruit "mystery speakers" who provide students clues to match a place/era/event they are studying.

- Take virtual field trips to portions or several portions of a few museums that highlight a person, era, or visual art under study. If you can do a Skype interview with a character from a museum of interactive display, all the better.

- Talk with experts or people living in the areas or situations you're studying to bring content to life. Allow students to ask them questions.

Simply connecting two parties isn't enough, though. Make sure you prepare your students and scaffold their way to a successful digital discussion or interview. For instance, discuss the following concepts:

- the importance of dress or appearance, even online

- how to practice the skill of looking at both the screen when listening and the camera while speaking

- the same use of skills and techniques for an in-person interview, as well as discussion practices and expectations when talking with peers in virtual conversations

- how to follow school "child safe" protocols (no use of last names), especially if you are connecting with other classes or groups of individuals outside your school community

Read More: "10 Tips for Great Classroom Video Calls" DitchThatTextbook.com/skypetips

TWITTER

Although it's considered a social-media tool, Twitter can become a powerful interactive learning instrument in the right hands. Creating a Twitter username, called a "handle," with a smartphone opens a world (literally) of possible connections and interactions. Start a prompt and add what's called a "hashtag" (the pound sign) to your tweets so that your students can find it. Students can contribute their own thoughts to the discussion by using the same hashtag. Twitter also adds some extra functionality to online discussions that other apps don't have, such as the ability to add video, cite sources, and more. Check out the current discussions about this book by searching for *#ditchbook* on Twitter as an example.

Read More: "A Blueprint for Twitter and Cell Phones in class from Joe Marquez" DitchThatTextbook.com/twitterclass

KNOW YOUR TWITTER LINGO

If you plan on using Twitter in your classroom, make sure you are up to date on the most common Twitter verbiage:

- **Hashtag**: The # symbol summarizes a tweet or connects it to a larger trend or discussion topic.
- **"Just 'At' Me"**: By putting @ before another person's Twitter handle, you can talk to that person directly. (Your message will show up as a notification for them.)
- **Subtweet**: You tweet about someone or something *without* "atting" them or without using a hashtag.

If Twitter still seems like a foreign language to you, don't worry! Check out the free ebook, *A Beginner's Guide to Twitter for Educators*. You'll be up to speed and tweeting in no time! (DitchThatTextbook.com/twitterebook)

PHOTOMATH

Using a smartphone, students can scan a math, geometry, or physics problem, and Photomath will show students the solution. When many teachers learn of this app, they want to try to ban its use. The reality is many students know about apps like Photomath, so ignoring its existence doesn't solve any problems. A more fruitful approach is to show students how to use tools like Photomath effectively and with a purpose.

Obviously, these kinds of apps should be used carefully and at specific times, such as when modeling a problem or after students have demonstrated their understanding of the necessary mathematical or scientific skill. Students don't learn by simply scanning math problems, but if the use of PhotoMath is accompanied by reflective prompts, such as the ones below, it can help to develop problem-solving, processing, and better reflection in learners. Organize the discussion in such a way that learners scaffold one another's thinking or so that you model critical problem-solving.

Possible Photomath Prompts

- Now that I see the answer, I wonder why . . .

- Once I compare my answer to the correct one, I see that . . .

- After I have seen the answer, I think something went wrong in the problem-solving process when . . .

- The best thing I did in reaching a solution on this problem was . . .

Other B.A.D. Museum Exhibitor Options

- **Verso (versolearning.com):** collaborative discussions online

- **Socrative (socrative.com):** quick anticipatory sets or assessments

- **Spiral (spiral.ac):** quick anticipatory sets and collaborative work with ability to send back student work

- **Google Slides (slides.google.com):** try using it to make choose-your-own-journey stories (see Chapter C for more on how)

B.A.D. Restaurant Owner

Even if you are the only computer user in the classroom, you can provide options for student choice when it comes to the learning process. You'll notice that the options that follow are grouped by purpose. Start by offering students a choice between two tools, then increase the number of options as you and your students feel more comfortable.

ANTICIPATORY SETS AND ASSESSMENTS

FLIPGRID, VOICETHREAD, AND GOOGLE VOICE

FLIPGRID (FLIPGRID.COM)

We described in Chapter I how Flipgrid can serve as a highly effective means of authentic interaction between you and your students or among your students. Flipgrid, VoiceThread, and Google Voice are "app"etizers that can be used by a student or groups of students on a mobile device quite effectively for performance-based assessment. These tools allow students to choose how they will express their knowledge.

VOICETHREAD (VOICETHREAD.COM)

This app provides an interesting platform where students can post video, auditory, or text-based comments about a piece of media you post. This media and the type of response given can vary widely, depending on what you choose as the basis of your discussion. Even if students aren't working at a level where they can create their own thread, you can identify a few publicly shared threads on which they can comment. This allows them to hear other learners' thinking.

GOOGLE VOICE (VOICE.GOOGLE.COM)

Google Voice, part of the G Suite, wasn't originally designed for educational uses, but you can repurpose it for educational assessments. Setting up a Google Voice number (free) that students can call and leave messages on can serve as a unique way to collect students' work. Imagine students "calling in" a foreign language assignment or work of poetry. This new means of expressing their knowledge can be very engaging!

CHOICE-OF-PROCESS TECH FOR OTHER PARTS OF YOUR LESSON

Limited classroom tech doesn't mean limited student choice. Every student learns and makes content differently. A B.A.D. classroom gives them that flexibility.

How can you build in choice when students have to rely on the teacher's tech or share in a small group? When students know what apps and options are available, they can pick the right tool for the job based on interest, preference, or a willingness to explore new options.

Think of it like a carpenter building a house. He or she has a box full of tools. The carpenter knows which tools are available and what each tool does. Based on the carpenter's vision for the project, he or she can save time and do a better job by selecting the right tool. Help students build their digital toolboxes by exposing them to a variety of useful apps and websites. You can help students by making suggestions. This means you should build your own toolbox too. You might also want to let students seek out and try tools on their own. A little guidance from you or a school or district tech leader can help students avoid potential pitfalls they might not foresee from their choices.

Reflect on this: How can you help students think through tech-tool choices before they start?

- **Piktochart (piktochart.com):** Create infographics and graphic design to demonstrate understanding. See an example here: dontditchtech.com/piktochart.

- **MindMup (mindmup.com):** Make mind maps to chart out concepts. See an example here: dontditchtech.com/mindmup.

- **YouTube playlists (youtube.com):** Curate (i.e. choose mindfully) videos to add to a playlist while explaining the thinking behind the choices. See an example here: goo.gl/uPX429. Tips for how to make a playlist: dontditchtech.com/playlist.

- **PowToons (Powtoon.com):** You and your students can use templates to create "ads" that summarize their understanding of content to create cartoons and presentations that are very student-friendly and engaging.

- **Blabberize (Blabberize.com):** Students can take any image and turn it into a talking object. This site might be good for younger students or shorter student-created summaries.

- **Digital textbooks (DitchThatTextbook.com/moresources):** Create them yourself based on the unique needs of your students *or* remix existing ones. See an example here: dontditchtech.com/testexample. Get a template here: dontditchtech.com/texttemplate.

OTHER B.A.D. RESTAURANT OWNER OPTIONS

- **PicCollage (pic-collage.com):** Create and modify pictures with backgrounds, additives, and more.

- **Educreations (educreations.com):** Create iPad-based interactive lessons that students can respond to.

- **Chatterpix (dontditchtech.com/chatterpix):** Makes photos and pictures talk. Literally!

Each of the resources above allow students to create something that demonstrates their understanding in the following ways: individually, as a small group, or as a class.

Example: If only the teacher has a device and is teaching the vocabulary for breakfast foods in German, students can describe their favorite breakfast foods in the new language. The teacher would use an image search (i.e., Google Images) to search for the foods based on the students' descriptions. Those images could be pulled into a PicCollage image collection. Likewise, students could use adjectives to describe their foods to a small group leader. The leader could sketch them on Educreations or pull a photo into a Google document or slide and label them with a small or large group. All these strategies build in student choice, whether the choice is inherent in the foods that students select, the app in which they are displayed, or the way in which they are labeled.

To ensure fair, consistent grades on assessments launched in varied platforms, make certain that your assessment is grounded in clear criteria and transparent thinking. You want to have a performance rubric or checklist that is platform-free, not platform-bound!

Check out a few of the rubrics that Nate uses for his multi-platform assessments in his World History and Dual Credit U.S. History courses as examples:

- World History (dontditchtech.com/whrubric)
- Dual Credit US History (dontditchtech.com/usrubric1)
- Dual Credit US History (dontditchtech.com/usrubric2)

B.A.D. Councilmember and Creative Art Coach

Both the Councilmember and the Creative Art Coach encourage students to drive the content focus. The key difference between the Councilmember and the Creative Art Coach is that the latter emphasizes metacognition. If you're already comfortable making this step, do so! Consider any app mentioned above in this chapter open for use and engage students in the process of deciding what to learn. If you aren't sure of the best ways to bring metacognition into a lesson, don't worry! We'll discuss how to get students thinking and driving the content choices in Chapter !, Teaching Kids to Reflect.

IDENTIFYING YOUR TECH SITUATION AND EXPLORING POSSIBILITIES

PART 2: CART/LAB

S tudents' access to school- or district-issued devices eliminates some of the challenges described in Part 1 of this chapter, but you will still deal with hassles. Consistency might be the greatest of them all. Sometimes the tablet cart isn't available. Some computers might not be working for some reason. And once you do get your hands on those devices, a few might be missing the programs or apps you need. In these challenging circumstances, what can a teacher do to differentiate effectively? Let's spend a few moments focusing on some possibilities.

FIRST THINGS FIRST

When working with carts and computer labs, follow a few "CUES" to make the whole process smoother:

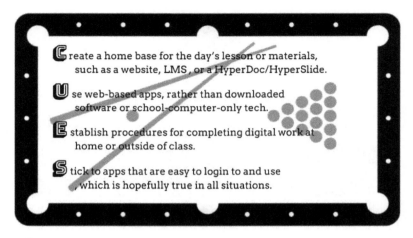

reate a home base for the day's lesson or materials, such as a website, LMS, or a HyperDoc/HyperSlide.

se web-based apps, rather than downloaded software or school-computer-only tech.

stablish procedures for completing digital work at home or outside of class.

tick to apps that are easy to login to and use, which is hopefully true in all situations.

CREATE A HOME BASE

Your time in a lab or with a computer cart is limited. That means it is important for students to access your warm-ups, activities, and other materials quickly and efficiently. Many elementary, second-ary, and post-secondary schools offer the use of a learning management system (LMS). Some examples are Canvas, Schoology, Moodle, and others. If you have one of these already, some of the work of organizing and distributing resources is done for you. If your school system doesn't use an LMS, you can easily make your own.

NATE'S TIP

If your school requires you to use a specific LMS, definitely do so. Even within an LMS's parameters, you can effectively distribute content in different ways to provide a streamlined and differentiated learning experience for your students. For example, if you have to create your assignments within an online module, consider creating a student-friendly HyperDoc for each day's lesson plan.

Google Classroom or Google Sites (classroom.google.com or sites.google.com)

With a free Google account, you can create a Google Classroom or Google Site that can serve as a sort of "diet LMS." Google Classroom offers some extended functionality over a Google Site. For example, you can send out announcements, create a class calendar, and do basic grading in Google Classroom. However, both of these free tools can fulfill the task of a digital hub for your students. They're quite easy to set up, customize, and use. Either (or both) might serve as a possible option for a teacher whose district does not provide a content-focused LMS.

> **Read More:** "The Google Classroom Quick-Start Guide + Tips and Tricks!" DitchThatTextbook.com/classroomquickstart

HyperDocs and HyperSlides

Word documents and Slides have been around for some time, but educators have really perfected the practice of turning them into educational resource distributors. Usually Google-based, HyperDocs and HyperSlides are easy to share and, if done correctly, make accessing lesson material easy and interactive.

Angie's Advice

If you're looking to jazz up your Google Slides or PowerPoint presentations, I highly recommend checking out the site "SlidesCarnival" (slidescarnival.com). The owner, Jimena Catalina, provides free templates for you to add or download. Her slides are easily customizable and look great!

What's the difference between HyperDocs and HyperSlides? Not much. They both feature a student-paced workflow and are based on great learning theory and instructional design. HyperDocs are created in a document; HyperSlides are created in slide presentation apps like Google Slides or PowerPoint.

When deciding between documents and Slides:

- Choose whatever format best fits your activity or your style.

- Documents are more linear in nature, i.e., you type text in a line, and the text flows straight down the page.

- Slides allow for more design freedom.

- With documents, you can organize content by breaking sections with page breaks and lines. In Slides, you can organize content by slide.

Quality HyperDocs or HyperSlides have many important parts, but getting started isn't too difficult. Check out these few examples that you could adapt for use in your own classroom:

- **HyperDoc example (dontditchtech.com/1950):** 1950's Civil Rights Movement

- **HyperSlide example (dontditchtech.com/moses):** Moses and the Israelites

Read More: Lots of helpful resources are available from the creators of HyperDocs, educators Lisa Highfill, Kelly Hilton, and Sarah Landis. Here are some to check out:

- the official HyperDocs website: HyperDocs.co
- a great how-to page with videos and descriptions: dontditchtech.com/hdhowto
- templates you can copy and customize to create your own HyperDocs: dontditchtech.com/hdtemp
- dozens of expertly-crafted HyperDocs shared by educators: HyperDocs.co/samples

A Quality HyperDoc or HyperSlide Should:

- share the day's lesson and objectives
- provide links to content, activities, and assessments, especially ones sourced online
- differentiate using those resources, especially through interactive apps that provide students a choice over process and content
- provide a common place where students can turn in work, such as by submitting links inside a Google Form or turning in work to Google Drive or Dropbox
- look good and seem well-themed (less important than the previous four points)

You can easily share a HyperDoc or HyperSlide via the blue "Share" button in Google Apps. It's also a smart idea to shorten that URL if you plan on displaying it for students to type into their devices. Some examples include Bitly (bitly.com) and TinyURL (tinyurl.com).

GOOGLE DRIVE AND DROPBOX
(DRIVE.GOOGLE.COM OR DROPBOX.COM)

Although not completely necessary for a Cart/Lab teacher to use, these applications make it easy to distribute and collect student work quickly when students do not have regular access to a device. Google Drive and Dropbox work very similarly: Students can download from or upload resources to an online folder. This lets students access materials online any time. You can also create a folder so that students can upload and turn in work for grading.

GOOGLE FORMS (FORMS.GOOGLE.COM)

An alternative way for students to turn in digital work is Google Forms, a survey tool to gather data from students (or anyone). In Nate's classes, he collects homework to a centralized location by asking students to submit a shareable link to their work inside the form. Here's how:

1. Create a Google Form (forms.google.com).

2. Add directions and the questions necessary to gather the data from students. (Be sure to include a short-answer question called "Name" for students' names *and* a short-answer question called "Link" where students paste the shareable link to their work.)

3. Decide if you want students to access the form while logged into their school Google accounts (if they have them). While editing your form, click the "Settings" gear icon and find the check box under the "General" tab that says "Restrict to users in …" your organization. Leave it checked if you want students to be logged in to their school Google accounts when they submit the form. Uncheck it if you don't want that extra step *or* if you're providing the

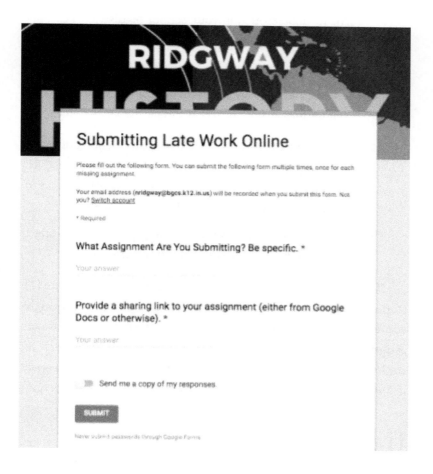

Nate's Tip

You can also usse Google Forms in a whle variety of ways to assist your teaching. For instance, I use it in my classroom to establish a common submission point for digital late work.

form to people outside your school or district, i.e., parents, community.

> **Note:** If you're using a standard Google account that wasn't provided by your school or district, this won't be an option.

4. Share the form with students using the "Send" button in the top right corner. Click the link icon and copy the URL to share with students. (Use the "Shorten URL" button to make an easily typable short URL if you'd like.)

5. Distribute the link to students using your LMS, Google Classroom, a short URL, or something else.

Two benefits to using Forms for collecting student work are (1) students can submit their work without registering for a Google account (when you uncheck the box in step three); (2) you can assign grades inside Google Forms and distribute them back to students; and 3) you can easily, without tons of emails and paper, tell which students have turned in work and which ones have not.

USE WEB-BASED APPS

When using tech in the classroom, nothing feels worse than the moment when things go wrong. To help reduce problems, eliminate—as much as possible—the need for your students to use apps that are only accessible on lab devices. Although there's definitely something to be said about the quality of software vs. online applications, the ultimate barrier to learning here is access. A school-only app might be wonderful in the lab, but if neither you nor your students can easily use it, what's the point of limiting yourself? In all likelihood, another app on the web can probably do exactly what your school's software program does but with greater flexibility and without the need to monitor loaded software issues.

Establish Expectations and Procedures for Online Work

Once your lesson has concluded in the lab or students have returned their devices, what do you need to do to make sure homework can be completed?

- Do not assign homework on days when a Cart/Lab was used.

- Adapt online work to be completed on paper as well as at a later time.

Let's say you do decide on option two. Unfortunately, you still face a slew of issues:

- First, can the homework assignment replicate the same skills that students were utilizing digitally?

- If yes, will the assignment ensure students are appropriately and equally supported outside of school?

- What if students only partially completed their assignment? Can they possibly transfer that work to paper? What if they need to turn in both digital and physical work?

Our advice: Consider ditching homework altogether. If you haven't taken that leap yet, check out *Ditch That Homework* by Matt Miller and Alice Keeler.

Stick to Apps that Are Easy to Use

With your students possibly on a different device every time they visit the lab or when you get ahold of a cart, it's especially important to minimize access issues in order to maximize learning time. When possible, avoid apps with lots of barriers for students to overcome in order to use them, such as:

- creating accounts

- logging in with usernames or passwords

- updating computer software, such as Adobe Flash Player

- downloading large or multiple files

Keep the theme "less is best" in mind. Try sticking to a few apps until both you and your students get the swing of the technology. Take a look at the sample classrooms below and the difference between using two different apps, Classtime and Verso, for the same warm-up. Assuming this is the first time the apps are used, notice the list of steps that students in Ms. Cheyenne's room must execute compared to her colleague:

Ms. Cheyenne's Room

Steps for App Used: Classtime (classtime.com)
1. Student clicks on the posted and distributed link.
2. Student enters name.
3. Student begins work on his or her warm-up and submits it.

Mr. Keegan's Room

Steps for App Used: Verso (versolearning.com)
1. Student clicks on the posted and distributed link.
2. Student clicks "Sign Up."

3. Student clicks "Student" for his or her account.
4. Student creates a username.
5. Student creates a password.
6. Student enters class code provided by teacher.
7. Student enters first and last name.
8. Student clicks the warm-up.
9. Student begins work on his or her warm-up and submits it.

This is not to say that Classtime is an inherently better app than Verso. When operating in the context of a Cart/Lab teacher, however, Classtime makes more sense to use due to its relatively simple logistics.

When it comes to planning your lessons as a Cart/Lab teacher, don't be afraid to take a quick look around the web for alternatives to an app you might typically use. It might save you time that you'd rather be spending with your students. And if you have tech-savvy colleagues or you follow techies on Twitter, ask them!

Remember to stick to the CUES if you are a Cart/Lab teacher:

- Create a "home base" your students can use to quickly get to material.

- Use online and cloud-sourced apps rather than downloadable software.

- Establish expectations and procedures for online work.

- Stick to apps that are easy to use.

PLANNING AND ADAPTING YOUR LESSONS WITH CART/LAB

CART/LAB PILOTS

As a Pilot in a Cart/Lab, you'll want to especially focus on the two themes we discussed at the beginning of the chapter: Keep your apps online and make sure they are easy to use. Start small, *poco a poco*, and build up your classroom's tech skills and tool kit gradually.

ANTICIPATORY SETS AND ASSESSMENTS

EDPUZZLE (EDPUZZLE.COM)

Edpuzzle is an easy way to take a creative video and captivate your learners' attention or assess their prior knowledge. It not only houses its own videos but lets you pull in media from other sites. For use in a Cart/Lab situation, you will have to provide students with an Edpuzzle link. This can be done via HyperSlide or HyperDoc, or just display it on the whiteboard. Remind students to bring earbuds if they are listening in a group setting.

CLASSTIME (CLASSTIME.COM)

Classtime can be a lifesaver in terms of gearing up students for an engaging lesson or for gathering assessment data. As its creators describe it, "Classtime is a solution for classrooms that complements in-class teaching with immediate feedback on students' level of understanding." Classtime features many prefabricated classroom challenges and spaces for teachers to import their own, unique questions. And what's handy for the lab or cart-based arrangement(s) is that no logins are ever needed. Simply put your Classtime session code at students' fingertips and have them start.

Socrative (socrative.com)

For all things assessment, consider Socrative. From Space Races to individual and differentiated questions (vary the versions of questions), Socrative can house your student roster, launch your assessment, and display student performance data. In a Cart/Lab situation, Socrative shines with its no-download necessary platform and simple login via Room Code.

Apps for the Rest of Your Lesson

Google Drive and G Suite

As we mentioned earlier, ease of use is a prime concern for a teacher in a Cart/Lab situation. Once your students have made a free Google account, the Google app suite can be a great way to quickly and easily share everything from activities to entire units with your students.

Prezi (prezi.com)

The app Prezi has been around for a while, but also consider it as another viable alternative for sharing resources with students. They're easy to share, and as long as they are designed well, students can easily find material you've embedded for them. Think of it as an LMS with a bit more of an artistic flair.

Iorad (iorad.com)

If you've ever had to explain a complicated step-by-step tech or online process to a student, which happens regularly in a computer lab, and then found yourself repeating it for another student just a few minutes later, you might want to take a look at iorad. It's a tutorial builder but quite a bit different—and much better—than giving students a step-by-step handout.

Because iorad creates online-based tutorials, it makes them so much more than a GIF or numbered points; iorad produces a step-by-step, clickable tutorial that feels just like the real website, document, or other digital doodad you're doing with your students.

You can make the tutorials interactive (Hey, Restaurant Owners!) by creating custom pathing, including hyperlinks, and embedding your tutorials in other apps. With the paid account version, you can also record accompanying audio.

NATE'S EXAMPLE

Try out this sample iorad Nate created for his Dual Credit U.S. History Class: dontditchtech.com/iorad.

OTHER CART/LAB PILOT OPTIONS

- **YouTube (youtube.com):** an online platform for video

- **Boseman Science (bozemanscience.com):** Hundreds of science-based instructional videos

- **Google Arts and Culture (artsandculture.google.com):** warehouse of digital artifacts and sources

- **Canva (canva.com):** User-friendly online graphic design

- **Piktochart (piktochart.com):** User-friendly online infographic design

Cart/Lab Museum Exhibitor

As you might recall, the Museum Exhibitor promotes interactivity at a level beyond that of the Pilot. Even if you are in a Cart/Lab scenario, there is lots of potential for student interaction.

Anticipatory Sets and Assessments

Spiral (spiral.ac)

Spiral is an innovative take on formal or informal assessments. As its name suggests, Spiral features a written or drawn assessment tool based on revision. Students can interactively respond to a prompt, and you can send feedback back to them for revisions. The app also features a decently quick login system for students, making it ideal in a Cart/Lab environment. The free version is excellent, but Spiral also offers a pro version at $50 annually that contains some additional benefits, such as deeper data tracking and more collaborative student activities.

Pear Deck or Nearpod (peardeck.com or nearpod.com)

If you're ready to add interactive elements to your in-class presentations, look no further than these two apps. Both allow you to upload your content material and then integrate warm-up questions, videos, outside content, assessments, and much more. Students simply use a code to access an open session you've established, and off they go! Nearpod also offers its own similar take on a "Teachers Pay Teachers" marketplace, where educators of any content area can purchase lessons for their own use. Please note that many of the features of Pear Deck and Nearpod are only accessible with the paid versions, but the free editions are worth checking out.

Read More: "20 Ways to Use Pear Deck to Engage Students"
DitchThatTextbook.com/peardeck

Interactive Apps for the Rest of Your Lesson

VideoNot.es (videonot.es)

If you've assigned your students a video to watch in class on YouTube or another platform, VideoNot.es is a great way to add in comprehensive, interactive note-taking. The app, once synced with Google Drive, allows students to create shareable, time-linked notes. Best of all, it's free! When students work independently in a lab, this is a must-have tool.

Nate's Example

Try out this sample VideoNot.es that Nate created
for his Dual Credit U.S. History Class:
dontditchtech.com/videonotes.

Google Slides Presenter View Audience Tool (slides.google.com)

A lesser-known feature of Google Slides, the Presenter View Audience Tool is perfect for the teacher who wants to elevate interactivity with his or her Google Slides but doesn't want the hassle of using a third-party app like Pear Deck or Nearpod. Students can pose questions, and the presenter can respond. One nice feature is that students' questions can be "voted up" or "voted down" by their peers so that teachers can prioritize what their students want to know most. If you'd like to check out this tool for yourself, see the following instructions.

1. Click the small arrow next to the present button.

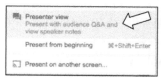

2. Click "Presenter View"

3. Select "Audience Tools" and click "Start New" to begin an Audience Q&A Session.

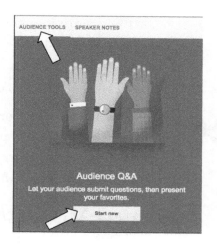

INSERT LEARNING (INSERTLEARNING.COM)

Insert Learning is a Chrome extension that allows teachers to embed interactive, differentiation tools (assessments, videos, text, Flipgrids, etc.) in online texts. It's free to use, and students can do everything with it, from collaborative idea crowdsourcing to individual writing annotations. Setup requires a few steps, including creating classes, lessons, and distributing student logins. But once you've got it going, it can be a pretty powerful app in your educator toolbox.

OTHER CART/LAB MUSEUM EXHIBITOR OPTIONS

- **Geogebra (geogebra.org):** free online math tools and apps

- **Gizmos (explorelearning.com):** math and science simulations

- **Textivate (textivate.com):** Create interactive games based on short texts

Cart/Lab Restaurant Owner

A Cart/Lab Restaurant Owner is looking to "serve up" different options for students to process content, so you'll notice that the apps that follow are multi-purposed. Think of it as replacing your hammer with a Swiss-Army knife.

Anticipatory Sets and Assessments

Drawings (docs.google.com/drawings)

Drawings is a versatile G Suite app. Use it as an assessment tool by having students create images, lines, arrows, shapes, and text boxes as responses. Just like Google Docs, you can distribute Drawings templates to students for customized, multi-media responses.

> **Read More:** "Ditch That Textbook's Google Drawings Manifesto" dontditchtech.com/drawings

Matt's Google Share URL Tricks

Making simple changes to Google Share URLs can really change how you distribute documents and other files. Here are just a couple of examples:

- **Auto-Copy:** Make the user automatically make a copy of the document you've shared with them, which is really useful for template sharing. *How*: Change the word "edit" in the share URL to the word "copy."

- **Auto-Present:** Make the user automatically enter presentation mode in a Google Slides file. This means that they can't see the other Slides in the presentation, which can be useful for Choose-Your-Own Adventure Games, hiding Slide notes, or holding back content for a dramatic reveal. *How*: Change the word "edit" in the share URL to the word "present."

Padlet (padlet.com)

We'll talk more in later chapters about how to use Padlet as a source for fostering student creativity and brainstorming (check out Chapter ! to learn more), but for our Restaurant Owners, think of utilizing Padlet in your room as a sort of LMS where you can offer students a "menu" of options on how to interact with content. Padlets are also easily shareable, making them ideal for the teacher stuck in a lab or using a cart.

Classkick (classkick.com)

Think of Classkick as another alternative to PearDeck or NearPod. Just like those apps, Classkick gives your students a variety of ways to respond to lessons, activities, assessments, or any kind of learning in your classroom. Once students log in with a code, Classkick offers a lot of functionality to play with, especially for iPad users.

Choice-of-Process Tech for Other Parts of Your Lesson

ThingLink (thinglink.com/edu)

We'll mention ThingLink later in Chapter ! for use as a creative tool, but when offering a variety of options to students as to how they can process content, Thinglink can serve as an exciting visual or artistic alternative to a HyperDoc or HyperSlide. Check out this example: dontditchtech.com/thinglink. Imagine the possibilities!

Dotstorming (dotstorming.com)

Dotstorming is an up-down voting system where student groups can vote for posted ideas called "cards." In the case of a Restaurant Owner in a Cart/Lab situation, think of using this app as a way for students to brainstorm or choose the learning processes that work best for them. The free account only comes with one board for you and your students to use, but in the right hands, Dotstorming can empower students to drive their own educational experiences.

VoiceThread (voicethread.com)

This app creates a media-intense platform where students can post video, auditory, or text-based comments about a wide variety of material. You can create your own at first as a teacher, but it becomes even more awesome when students can start making their own. Even if you first use your VoiceThread, though, this app prides itself on students sharing their thinking: commenting, collaborating, critiquing, etc. It also has excellent mobile apps and can be used by any device with a keyboard, although a microphone and webcam really open up its true potential.

Other Cart/Lab Restaurant Owner Options

- **Wheel Decide (wheeldecide.com):** item or random student selector
- **StickPick (dontditchtech.com/stickpick):** iPad-based random student selector
- **The Brainstormer (dontditchtech.com/brainstormer):** select random plots, subjects, settings, for creative writing. available both as an app for purchase and for free online

Cart/Lab Councilmember and Creative Art Coach

Like we did with Part 1 of this chapter (the B.A.D. section), we've combined the options for Councilmember and Creative Art Coach. We'll talk all about metacognition and student-driven content in some later chapters, but if you're ready to start putting those in place through tech, do it! Consider any app mentioned in the second half of this chapter fair game. Here are a couple of specific examples:

Cart/Lab Councilmember

We just mentioned Thinglink (thinglink.com) as a way for Restaurant Owners to help their students have input on the learning *process*. However, it can also be used by teachers to easily distribute a variety of options on classroom *content*. Create a Thinglink and add several diverse "bubbles" of discussions, videos, activities, etc., that grab all your students' different interests. If you'd like an example on how to do this, check out this example here: dontditchtech.com/bubbles.

Creative Art Coach

Using a Dotstorm (dotstorming.com), have students decide on the content that will be reviewed during a study session, then use it so that students can reflect on their learning by making comments on particular posts. Because there's no login information necessary to access it, a shared Dotstorm makes a perfect Cart/Lab companion. Nate does this in his World History and Dual Credit U.S. History classes, especially before large quizzes or tests. Check out his example here: dontditchtech.com/dotstorm.

MATT'S REMINDER

We've discussed lots of new apps and strategies for their use. Rather than trying to incorporate all of them at once, make sure you limit the number of apps and sites that you use, especially at first. When there are too many tools, students become overwhelmed, and they spend too many instructional minutes learning how to use those tools instead of on the skills and content they need. If you can create new experiences with apps they're already familiar with, you spend more time on learning.

TAKING THEIR ATTENTION CAPTIVE

In this chapter—in fact, in the next four (T,C,H, and I)—we're going to examine how to use tech to differentiate your instruction. We'll be discussing quite a few apps, strategies, and examples that you can implement in your own classroom.

What's up first is a look at how to grab your students' attention as well as sustain it. Even without tech, attention is an absolute must-have. Imagine the learning process—or lack thereof—if you didn't have your kids' attention! Catching and maintaining their interest in our teaching should be as important to us as strong lesson design.

What we do know from the science of learning is that, at every stage of the learning process, attention is a central component in moving skills and content to the long-term memory. For us as practitioners, this means that we should not just seek to grab attention at the beginning of a lesson, but we should strive to keep our students engaged throughout our time with them. What good is a warm-up if the students can't remember anything from the rest of the class period?

In the well-regarded Information Processing Model of learning, attention is a central component that facilitates the movement of stimuli from the senses to the working and long-term memory.

The Information Processing Model

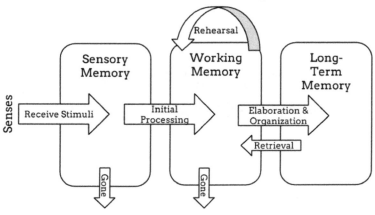

In simple terms, where every arrow moves horizontally in the model, a student must be *attending* in order to remember the content and, thus, learn! This attention is created through our instructional design.

And now that we have *your* attention, let's talk about the ways to use technology to captivate and keep your students' interests. We have divided attention-captivating strategies into the areas that speak to students' own cultural experiences and developmental needs. Culturally Responsive Teaching is a pedagogy that recognizes the importance of including students' cultural references in all aspects of learning; for instance, when students' own lived experiences or preferences are included in lesson design, attention peaks. Just like us adults, students like to know that their preferences are valued.

A meaningful intersection between the inclusion of students' lived experiences and teen culture is found in the following ideas for captivating attention.

Let's take a look at the following chart where we show how one application can be used by teachers of all skill levels to facilitate a specific kind of attention-getter.

Oh, and don't worry. A number of apps can fulfill the same function as those below. Just like with any technology and teaching, how you use them is what matters.

Attention!

Five Ideas for Creating Captivating Experiences in Class

1. **Personalization and Choice**
The start of the lesson or lesson segment is based on students' explicit choices.

2. **Pop Culture**
What's new today attracts students' attention. How can the latest music, videos, novels, and pop culture be integrated into the start of your lesson?

3. **Controversy and Ambiguity**
When students approach critical thinking, they like to debate and argue. Add school-appropriate controversy. This also promotes rigor: there's no one answer!

4. **Mystery**
Who doesn't like a good mystery? Leading students into the unknown can grab their attention.

5. **Disruption**
Now, you can turn the tables on the debaters. How can you challenge students' preconceived ideas or existing knowledge?

	Personalization	Pop Culture	Controversy and Ambiguity	Mystery	Disruption
How	Find a place that holds personal meaning for students.	Explore posts from social media accounts and use **these** to embed pop culture.	Grab engaging speakers to peak students' interest about a topic.	Explore the unknown or a baffling situation that captivates student interests.	Display countervailing media that is connected to your lesson.
Example of Tech Used	Google Maps — maps.google.com [QR code]	Twitter — twitter.com [QR code]	Ted Talks — ted.com [QR code]	AirPano — airpano.com [QR code]	Memes. Various Sites. Just make sure your students are following digital citizenship expectations you set for your classroom!
Pilot	Teacher highlights local landmark.	Teacher explores current trend or account.	Teacher presents Ted Talk as a whole-group activity.	Teacher chooses an unnamed photo to pique student interests. Teacher-prompted questions or sentence stems follow.	Teacher chooses meme and one standard way to process reaction and excitement.

Museum Exhibitor	Teacher creates an interactive map and photo tour.	Teacher displays a few trends for students to review.	Teacher presents Ted Talk as whole group, but students may choose discussion from stations activity.	Teacher distributes 360° videos to students' mobile and personal devices, and w/teacher support, students generate connections.	Students edit a pre-selected meme to address as a class or in small groups.
Restaurant Owner	Student chooses between writing or drawing about a local landmark.	Student chooses between composing a picture-based or written-based tweet.	Student chooses between debating, writing, or sketching a reaction to a Ted Talk.	Student chooses between the creation of a written response, a role play, or an illustration about a puzzling photograph.	Students vote on a meme that best challenges a well-known concept or myth.
Council member	Teacher provides regional analysis or choice of predetermined landmarks and tours.	Teacher offers a choice between several trends to analyze.	Teacher offers students a choice between two to three **TED Talks** with similar content.	Students analyze a few incomplete photographs of their choice; analysis used to drive further discussion.	Students create a meme that disrupts thinking or perceptions about topic or concept.
Creative Art Coach	Choice of geographic area that meets established criteria.	Create a class hashtag and submit their own trends to discuss and explore.	Create a Ted Talk (or one-minute creative summary) as reaction to such.	Teacher shares a provocative question about a few photos related to the concept, and students must determine how question(s) connect to photos.	Students create a meme that disrupts thinking or concept. At end of lesson, students revise previously used memes with feedback from teacher and peers.
Other Possible Apps	Tourbuilder. withgoogle.com 360cities.net	Instagram.com Snapchat.com Marco Polo Newseum.org newspapermap.com Ditty	Specific YouTube Channels Podcasts	Skype Mystery Calls (arranged by teacher)	Adam Ruins Everything MythBusters

Personalization by a Pilot

Find a place that holds personal meaning for students. Grab photos, places, or videos of their lived world to integrate their community and culture(s) into your lessons.

Example: Nate teaches a dual credit U.S. History class in Indianapolis and used this local example of eugenics to connect to student's lives.

Link: dontditchtech.com/eugenics

Pop Culture by a Museum Exhibitor

Spark students' interest in your lesson by utilizing collections of posts from social media accounts. Using Twitter, the teacher provides links to interactive, multi-media, Twitter moments.

Example: This Twitter moment of Venezuela's 2018–2019 election really shows how this media combines audio, pictures, and video from multiple perspectives.

Link: dontditchtech.com/election

Nate's Tip

Besides curated moments that have already been made, teachers and students can create ones for their own use too.

Link: dontditchtech.com/curate

Controversy and Ambiguity by a Restaurant Owner

Student chooses between debating, writing, or sketching a reaction to a TED Talk.

> **Example**: America has a pretty complicated relationship with the rest of the world, to say the least. Using archetypes, students were able to have either a whole-group or small-group scaffolded discussion about this controversial topic after watching a Ted Talk.

> **Link:** dontditchtech.com/archetypes

Mystery by a Councilmember

Students analyze a few incomplete photographs of their choice; once they've done this, they then analyze the revealed whole photograph and examine how seeing the entire picture changes the meaning of the picture or their understanding of it. This analysis is used to drive further discussion.

> **Example**: These photos pull from students' existing knowledge of Hitler, the Great Depression, and Europe's colonization of the Western Hemisphere.

> **Link:** dontditchtech.com/photos

Disruption by a Creative Art Coach

Students create a meme that disrupts thinking or perceptions about a topic or concept. At the end of the lesson, students revise their memes based on feedback from teacher and peers.

Example: The teacher challenges students to think about the idea of fish not existing. Look how promoting disequilibrium can prompt thinking!

Link: dontditchtech.com/fish

With those examples in mind, think about a lesson you've taught or will teach in your classroom. What type of tech-based attention-getter could you use to engage your students from bell to bell? A dash of mystery and suspense? A scene wrought with tension? A surprisingly stark statement? Give one a try!

CHANNELING THE REAL WORLD

J ust like the 1990's MTV phenomenon, *The Real World*, education has generally framed its subject matter, pedagogy, and attitude toward how it perceives content to connect to the true, outside world. Technology has drastically altered the way that human beings live in the twenty-first century. Commerce, social interaction, and the exchange of information have changed dramatically through the internet in ways that both sociologists and everyday citizens have yet to fully comprehend.

Despite the present-day tremendous access to information, images, and communication, the foundational pillars of the education system remain largely the same. Standards, high-stakes testing, ancillary materials, and print textbooks still drive much of our K–12 curricula. Thus, today we teachers find ourselves in a paradox:

How can we use these new, varied levels of technology to open our content to real-world experiences for our students when our systems are grounded in outmoded foundations? In other words, how do we make it real to the seven- to eighteen-year-olds who want to learn?

Authenticity of content, processes, and expression increases intrinsic motivation, which, we know from last chapter, promotes sustainable learning. This chapter will help you grow in your integration of technology in the classroom while increasing the authentic, real-world use of the content under study.

Each section below is specifically written (differentiated) to the needs of the roles of Pilots, Museum Exhibitors, Restaurant Owners, Councilmembers, and Creative Art Coaches. As you read through the section, look for ways to increase change and authenticity in your classroom.

PILOTS

You may be voyaging into the world of integrating technology into your classroom for the first time. With that in mind, many of the strategies mentioned below are aimed to rely upon both the strengths and skills of the non-technological world you've been comfortable with while straying off into some new experiences. Again, the aim here is to enhance your instruction, not replace it entirely. Here are ways you can take off!

GOOGLE EARTH (GOOGLE.COM/EARTH)

Google Earth is a fantastic example of an authenticity-based app to use in your classroom, mostly because it's about us, humans. Google Earth essentially employs Google Maps and then adds several extremely relevant features:

- Numerous informational layers can be used to examine anything from geography, weather, historical sites, and sightseeing tours.

- It can include in-person and satellite imagery of natural features, such as oceans, coral reefs, the Moon, and Mars.

- It can link to outside content for further exploration or study.

- It offers a new Tour Builder that you can use to create interactive, multimedia tours. It's a great way to push your own tech development onto the role of a Museum Exhibitor. You can get the link to it here: tourbuilder. withgoogle.com. If you'd like to see a sample tour, go to: dontditchtech.com/tourbuilder.

- The use of GeoGuessr as a great way to grab students' attention and embed authenticity. Your class can gather clues to figure out where in the world you have landed. Check it out at geoguessr.com/world/play.

Note: Google Earth is available for your web browser or as a desktop application.

Nate's Tip

Google Earth is particularly useful if you're a 6–12 social studies, science, or elementary school teacher. It's also great to use in a 1:1 classroom, as long as students are carefully monitored and directed. To really amp up the authenticity, try creating a problem-solution scenario based on something you and your students find together: geography, an instance of human-environment interaction, a piece of architecture, etc.

YouTube (YouTube.com)

YouTube has become an incredibly powerful educational source since its creation in 2005. Since most educators will already be familiar with YouTube, let's talk about how we can use it as Pilots more specifically, and as educators, use it wisely.

Content-wise, there are thousands of educational channels to explore, and most are easily Googleable. See "Angie's Arenas" for a list of her favorite YouTube resources.

Using YouTube—and using it well—as an authenticity-focused educator boils down to a few key guidelines:

- Students will begin to lose attention after long stretches of video (generally longer than five minutes).

- Students want to see videos that make connections to their own lives or present startling or remarkable information that challenges their thinking/assumptions.

- Don't send kids into "videoland" cold! Use previewing, knowledge-gathering strategies first to maximize learning. This helps viewing experiences to stick or move to the long-term memory and gives you a sense of existing knowledge.

Some preview sentence stems you might ask students to complete are:

- The title (topic) of this video is_____. What do you know about _____ from before this class?

- After reading the title, what do you predict this video is about?

- How do you think _____ looks on a screen? If you created a video about _____, what would you show others?

Angie's Arenas

Math
- Khan Academy—youtube.com/khanacademy
- Numberphile—youtube.com/user/numberphile

Social Studies
- Crash Course (several variations)—youtube.com/user/crashcourse

Science
- Bozeman Science—youtube.com/user/bozemanbiology
- MythBusters for the Impatient—youtube.com/user/mythbustersimpatient

English/Language Arts
- The Teaching Channel—teachingchannel.org/videos
- The Literacy Shed—literacyshed.com
- Crash Course (several variations)—youtube.com/user/crashcourse

P.E./Health
- "The Quest" Adapted Physical Education—dontditchtech.com/quest
- PHYSEDagogy Pedagogy for Physical Education—youtube.com/user/pegeeksunite

Performing Arts
- Smithsonian Videos—youtube.com/user/smithsonianchannel
- University of California Television—youtube.com/user/UCtelevision

VISUAL ARTS
- The Guggenheim Museum—
youtube.com/user/guggenheim
- Art 21 for Educators—youtube.com/user/art21org

MODERN LANGUAGE
- FluentU—dontditchtech.com/fluentu
- Easy Languages—youtube.com/user/magauchsein

BUSINESS AND TECHNOLOGY
- Stanford Graduate Business School—
youtube.com/user/stanfordbusiness/videos

POTPOURRI CHANNELS
- TED-Ed—youtube.com/user/TEDEducation

PODCASTS

Podcasts are an extremely useful source of information for building interest in class, previewing a subject, or assisting struggling readers or language learners. They bring authentic experts right into your classroom. You can access podcasts from a variety of sites, but Anchor, iTunes, Google Play Music, Overcast, and Spotify are some of the most common. Because of the huge variety of available podcasts, we recommend sticking to the guidelines we provided earlier in this chapter for YouTube.

MUSEUM EXHIBITORS

Being a Museum Exhibitor in the classroom means you strive to make your content interactive for the tourists who visit your displays. Allow your students to work and grapple with real-world content, personalities, problems, and examples in (digitally) tangible ways. Let's take a look at a few ways to get you started.

Skype, Facetime, and Google Hangouts

All three of these apps provide a variation on a theme of face-to-face interactive communication. Connection to the real world can greatly heighten student engagement and provide personally meaningful experiences. Consider taking virtual field trips, inviting guest speakers for video appearances, or connecting with other classes via Mystery Skype sessions. Of course, a lot goes into setting up these kinds of experiences, including preparing students for the interview, practicing discussion skills, and making sure everyone is clear about school policies on digital communication with staff, students, and outside professionals. But the impact is worth the effort!

Links:

- Skype.com
- Zoom (zoom.us)
- Facetime: available on only i-devices
- Find video call partners: SkypeInTheClassroom.com

`</html>`

Choose-Your-Own-Journey Stories via Google Slides (google.com/slides/about)

Did you know you can create Choose-Your-Own-Journey Stories with Google Slides? Yes! You can use this app to create the kinds of stories you read as a child, where you choose the ending based on which page you turned to. Creating a digital reading experience for students provides an unparalleled way for them to make their own decisions. Talk about interactive! Let the thinking begin!

On the following page, you'll find a few examples that Nate has used in his social studies classes as well as a tutorial where Nate can show you how to make your own stories.

How to Make Your Own
Choose-Your-Own Journey Stories:
dontditchtech.com/cyoa

Examples of Nate's Stories:
"A Tiny Dynasty"— dontditchtech.com/dynasty

NEARPOD AND PEAR DECK
(NEARPOD.COM AND PEARDECK.COM)

If you're ready to add **interactive** elements to your in-class presentations, look no further than Nearpod and Pear Deck. These apps allow you to upload your content material and then integrate warm-up questions, videos, outside content, assessments, and much more. In terms of **authenticity**, what could be more real than an integrated virtual reality tour of Mars (Nearpod) or drag-and-drop questions (Pear Deck) in your PowerPoint? Students simply use a code to log into an open session you've established, and off they go! Nearpod also offers its own similar take in a "Teachers Pay Teachers" marketplace, where educators of any content area can purchase lessons for their own use. Please note that many of the features of Nearpod and Pear Deck are only accessible with the paid versions, but the free editions still have lots to offer.

Read More: "20 Ways to Use Pear Deck to Engage Students" DitchThatTextbook.com/peardeck

VideoNot.es (videonot.es)

In combination with sites like YouTube (see our previous section on using YouTube with authenticity), VideoNot.es is a fantastic way to turn videos into an interactive educational experience and study tool. As its name suggests, this app allows students to take notes alongside a video. What makes it better than a companion notation page, however, is that VideoNot.es creates a time-link between your writing and the video itself, allowing for students to go back to the exact moment a new idea or concept was introduced. The notes also sync to Google Drive, which means that students can share and collaborate on notes they watch from a common video.

Restaurant Owner

An authentic Restaurant Owner offers students choice in both presentational and practice technologies as well as the interactivity utilized by Museum Exhibitors. Students' learning processes are varied based on their own needs and preferences.

You'll notice that a lot of apps are listed in this section. Don't worry about mastering each and every one. After all, most of our students are digital natives, and when we give them the right support and choice, we're handing them the menu and helping them select the kind of learning that works best for them.

Flipgrid (flipgrid.com)

Flipgrid adds collaboration, interaction, choice, and discovery to videoconferencing. When you create a "Grid," students can post their own face-based video and post comments and feedback on their peers' creations. New discussions will spawn from their posts (both with their peers and with educational communities from around the world.) Since it's so flexible and adaptable to any content area, Flipgrid is a great addition to any classroom seeking to add that extra dose of *realness* to students' lives.

> ***Read More:*** "Catch the Flipgrid Fever! 15+ Ways to Use Flipgrid in Your Class" DitchThatTextbook.com/flipgrid

StoryMap (storymap.knightlab.com)

Providing options for students to interact with presentations outside of hyperlinked Google Slides, Prezi, or Nearpod takes a bit of creativity. If you've wanted to tell the real story of a place, person, or event, StoryMap could be one of several choices to consider.

Below, you'll find a few examples that Nate has used in his social studies classes as well as a tutorial for making your own maps. StoryMap isn't just for social studies though. Imagine the possibilities with English/language arts, world languages, science, and the visual arts.

Examples of Nate's StoryMaps:

- Two Perspectives on the Persian War
    - Perspective 1: dontditchtech.com/Persian1
    - Perspective 2: dontditchtech.com/Persian2
- The Voyages of Zheng He: dontditchtech.com/zheng

> ***Read More:*** "How to Make Your Own StoryMaps" dontditchtech.com/makecyoa

Penzu.com

For your more intrapersonal students, have them set hands-to-keyboard with Penzu, an online journal portal where they can present or process content. Via a link, students can share their brilliance with you or classmates. Penzu also allows the choice to import graphics, fonts, etc. See an example Angie drafted for her language classes at dontditchtech.com/penzu.

Other Restaurant Owner Apps

- **Photopeach (photopeach.com):** create free slideshows with music and captions

- **Educreations (educreations.com):** turns apple device into interactive whiteboard

- **VoiceThread (voicethread.com):** transforms media into interactive space

- **Quizlet (quizlet.com):** teacher/student-created practice platform

- **Khan Academy (khanacademy.org):** content-explanation site

- **Grammarly (grammarly.com):** automated grammar checker

Councilmember

In the role of Councilmember, the teacher creates an environment where "voters" (students) choose between "issues" (content) that the teacher provides. When discussing ways to differentiate tech as a means of increasing authenticity, content plays an especially key role.

The topic of differentiation of content has been thoroughly explored by educators. Here we'll look at ways to use tech devices, apps, and the real world to increase student choice. As you explore these options in your classroom, you'll see a positive effect on student motivation and learning outcomes.

TAKE A LOOK

To see differentiation of content and tech in action, check out this example from one of Nate's U.S. History lessons: dontditchtech.com/ush.

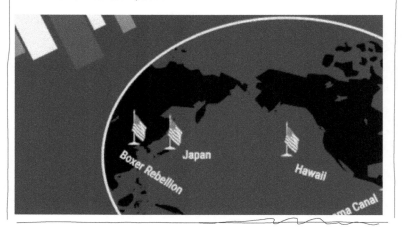

THE LITERACY SHED (LITERACYSHED.COM/HOME.HTML)

A multi-content exploratory site that focuses on English/language arts, the Literacy Shed provides videos, questions, explanations, and prompts for viewing authentic content. Angie has used this site to have students study various aspects of the holiday *El Día de los Muertos*, the Day of the Dead, with students analyzing context and audience through varied auditory, video, and text sources.

BBC iWONDER (BBC.CO.UK/IWONDER)

Although it's no longer being updated, BBC iWonder is a fascinating site on a multitude of global issues, ranging from arts to ethics and beyond. Because the articles are written on specific topics, consider using it in any classroom as a complementary resource for study.

BIE.org (bie.org/about)

Buck Institute is one of the primary sources for finding inspiration in student-driven or project-based learning (PBL). Even if you are not ready to go full force PBL, use the BIE website to find inspiration and resources as a menu of options for your students. Grade levels and content vary tremendously at BIE.org.

PowerMyLearning.org (powermylearning.org)

PowerMyLearning provides content playlists on a variety of subjects and materials, with most of them bent toward personalized learning. Full access comes with a district or school account, but quite a few, free, curated playlists are still available to individual educators. This also allows teachers to create playlists. Again, combine resources like this with material of your own and create some options!

Other Councilmember Apps

Because a Councilmember needs to provide a variety of places where students can interact with content, the apps and sites below can serve as additional, authentic content resources. Pair or combine them with the app mentioned above to create purposeful groupings.

- **iCivics (icivics.org):** free lessons and resources on civics education

- **Stanford History Education (sheg.stanford.edu):** free curriculum on civics and history education

- **Teaching Tolerance (tolerance.org):** materials centered on diversity and social justice

- **NBC Learn (nbclearn.com/portal/site/learn):** site focused on stories and current events and relevance to classroom subjects

- **TED-Ed (ed.ted.com):** quality animated videos on a variety of real-world problems and questions
- **Bozeman Science (bozemanscience.com):** videos for most high-level science courses
- **Smithsonian Videos (smithsonianchannel.com/videos):** clips on a wide spectrum of real-world subjects
- **American Museum of Natural History (science. amnh.org):** clips and resources on some natural history
- **Newseum (newseum.org/todaysfrontpages):** View current front pages of global newspapers
- **Oercommons.org (oercommons.org):** a free, public curriculum and content site
- **Annenberg Learner (learner.org):** lesson plans on a variety of subjects, kindergarten through college
- **Federal Reserve Bank of St. Louis (stlouisfed.org/education):** resources on economics education from the Bank of the U.S.

CREATIVE ART COACH

In this most divergent role from that of a Pilot, the teacher leaves the "sage-on-the-stage" role and transforms into the "guide on the side," offering students the most choice of all the decision-making processes related to learning. He or she creates a canvas, guided by standards and essential questions, and the students paint the picture. They are truly authors of their own learning!

The carpenter analogy mentioned earlier holds true here too. Students build familiarity with a variety of digital tools. They learn their strengths and weaknesses. When it's time for students to take charge of their learning, they can more easily envision next steps when they've assembled a varied digital toolbox.

The way you differentiate tech as a Creative Art Coach for authenticity is actually very similar to a Councilmember but with more emphasis on metacognition and student-driven content. We'll talk more about how you can use differentiated technology to reach this stage in Chapter H and Chapter !. For now, consider any of the apps or websites mentioned previously in this chapter to be well-suited for you as a Creative Art Coach.

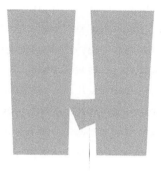

HOW TO EMPLOY TECH
TO VARY CONTENT

N umerous demands are placed on today's teachers. Not only do
we have to lead our students through a successful day, but we
also have to teach objectives, take students to lunch, make pho-
tocopies, address behavior concerns, attend professional development workshops, and take on everything else in between! In a
word, teaching can sometimes feel pretty chaotic. On top of all
that, we're expected to do this superhero thing called "differentiation" for our students.

In the previous chapters, we've given you an overview of tools
that will help you upgrade your teaching with differentiation.
We've talked about how to offer greater authenticity and how to
grab and maintain student attention. In this chapter, we're going
to get into the heart of the intersection of tech and differentiation.
But don't be intimidated or think it will be super theoretical—we'll
create a practical guide and handbook for you to use.

One expert on differentiation in the classroom, Carol Ann Tomlinson, writes, "The idea of differentiating instruction to accommodate the different ways that students learn involves a hefty dose of common sense as well as sturdy support in the theory and research of education. It is an approach to teaching that advocates active planning for student differences in classrooms."

In a carefully created approach, begin with a curriculum that establishes learning goals and use your pre/formative assessment processes so that differentiated instruction stays true to the learning outcomes. "Active planning for student differences" means that we have to do more than make our tech interactive (as a Museum Exhibitor) or provide options for students' best learning (as a Restaurant Owner). It means that we need to push our practice to the next level by using technology to differentiate the content of our classrooms.

SO WHAT'S NEW AT EACH LEVEL?

TEACHERS   STUDENTS

	Teacher			Student
	Pilot	Teacher-Led Technology	Passenger	
	Museum Exhibitor	Interactive Tech	Tourist	
	Restaurant Owner	Student-Chosen Process	Diner	
	Councilmember	Student-Chosen Content	Voter	
	Creative Art Coach	Student-Driven Content & Quality Feedback	Artist	

You'll notice that this chapter's topic, content differentiation, is first mentioned in the role of Councilmember. Thus, this chapter will be especially applicable to:

- Restaurant Owners who want to further improve on their practice and move on to become a Councilmember and

- Councilmembers and Creative Art Coaches who want to refine their skills.

If you're a Pilot or a Museum Exhibitor and feel left out, think about this chapter as a preview of what's to come, or better yet, an idea laboratory where you can experiment and grow. No matter where you are role-wise, don't forget to take small steps based on the ideas and suggestions ahead. Few benefits—and much frustration—await the teacher who tries to do everything all at once.

We suggest introducing one new idea, technique, or skill in a unit, evaluating and reflecting on how it went, and then trying it again in a couple of weeks. In short, differentiate for yourself in the same way you do for your students.

Getting Down To It

Matt has said, "There's no playbook for learning in today's classrooms," and the same holds true for differentiation. There is no one single lesson, activity, or project that perfectly captures the essence of differentiating content. Rather, we recommend thinking about doing so through three principles that can apply throughout your teaching. Try to make your teaching have some VIM: variety, intentionality, and meaning.

Variety

Intentionality

Meaning

Remember: *poco a poco!*

Although the best differentiated lessons and units will capture all three letters of VIM, you can feel good about just getting started in *one* area. That *one area* can serve as a solid foundation for building confidence and getting the hang of employing technology to support differentiation.

We're actually going to start out of order—and for good reason. *Intentionality* refers to the idea that a teacher differentiates with purpose rather than making modifications on the fly. This is especially true with technology. Lots of apps and devices are flashy or trendy, but why and how a tool is used matters more than what's hot at the moment.

What are some signs that you intentionally differentiate? Ask yourself, do you:

- consider specific grouping and other supports based on learners' needs?
- regularly make use of a toolkit of tricks, apps, and other differentiation-based tech because the predetermined inclusion of such will make the learning more accessible, authentic, or more customized for the students?
- utilize data and other student information to create and launch lessons and units?

Look at the abbreviated lesson plan from Angie that follows as an example of intentionally-designed differentiation of content.

The concept: "Family structure." Data from yesterday's, out-the-door, stoplight, Post-it note prompt indicates learners are in three levels:

- One group is just beginning to apply the vocabulary and needs additional practice.

- One group of learners knows the vocabulary with support and needs to be challenged by further application of the vocabulary, and

- One small group is ready to move on! They need elaboration, challenge, and more rigor within this objective.

Angie's Spanish 101 Lesson

Lesson Structure and Sequence

Concept: "Family Relationships"

Given a visual, I can correctly describe family members.

(Day 2 or 3 of lesson sequence)

Anticipatory Set: Play the video *"Canción de la familia"* with a stop at the first full photo as comprehensible input. Teacher and students pose comprehension questions. Circle and extend using vocabulary.

Play video: dontditchtech.com/familia

Differentiated rehearsal and elaboration based on group (color-coded) assignment. See orange column.

Differentiation

Group One: Given scaffolded visual note sheet with Spanish vocabulary for family members, students will apply vocabulary to complete questions in edPuzzle version of *"Canción de la familia."* Video at: dontditchtech.com/cancion.

Bloom's taxonomy: Recall or write

Group Two: With or without visual note sheet (based on student need), students will describe family relationships described in video clip (free choice of descriptions).

Video at: dontditchtech.com/relationships.

Bloom's taxonomy: Restate in own words

Group three: Given a photo of the Spanish royal family at dontditchtech.com/royal, students will correctly describe family members in their Penzu journal or on a Classtime.com link.

Bloom's taxonomy: Apply content in different context

Kyle Beimfohr, instructional technology coach from Zionsville Community Schools, has begun to incorporate VR in his science lessons for elementary students. The text set is differentiated by student need at Newsela, and the students' understanding is differentiated based on the format they choose.

KYLE'S ABBREVIATED WEATHERING AND EROSION UNIT: (ANTICIPATING AND REHEARSAL)

LESSON STRUCTURE AND SEQUENCE

Concept: "Weathering and Erosion"

Students will show understanding of differences between weathering and erosion and be able to give examples of each.

Anticipatory Set: Students will choose two non-fiction text articles about weathering and erosion from the text set to read at their Lexile level and take the quiz as an assessment.

Newsela Text Set: dontditchtech.com/newsela

Using a class set of VR headsets, have students explore the Grand Canyon using the Google Expeditions app. Show students examples of weathering and erosion found in the canyon.

- edu.google.com/expeditions/#explore

Differentiated assessment based on student choice. See orange column.

Differentiation

Group One: Use a presentation software to explain differences between weathering and erosion.

- PowerPoint
- Google Slides
- Prezi

Bloom's taxonomy: Remember and understand

Group Two: Create an infographic giving examples of different types of weathering and erosion providing data for each.

- piktochart.com

Bloom's taxonomy: Apply and analyze

Group three: Using a 360 camera, students will create a VR tour using Google Tour Creator showing examples of both weathering and erosion in their community.

- vr.google.com/tourcreator

Bloom's taxonomy: Apply and create

How to Get Started with Intentional Differentiation

- Consider the concept or skill to be taught.

- Think about what data you have readily available or can gather via a quick assessment (see Chapter I²). This might be just observational or anecdotal.

- Using that data, consider how learning might be improved by one or more of these:

  » What kind of grouping works best with your objective for the lesson? Think about scaffolding for diverse learners, for varied content, or for linguistic, language, and reading skill needs (more on how to help with these in the next section).

  » Does the data from pre-assessments or observations show that specific groups might be helpful when tackling your learning objective?

  » What instructional technologies have you learned about that might support specific learning needs? Does this influence grouping or flow?

  » How can particular technologies support your work as an instructional designer in varying content and the process of assessing learning?

Extensions and Other Applications for Intentional Differentiation:

Instructional Technology	How to Use this App
Socrative Link: socrative.com	Quickly gain pre-assessment or formative assessment data to inform lessons.
Kahoot Link: kahoot.it	
Quizizz Link: quizizz.com	
Go Pollock Link: gopollock.com	
Spiral Link: spiral.ac	
Plickers Link: plickers.com	
Gradecam Link: gradecam.com	
Wheel Decide Link: wheeldecide.com	Select random students or content (grouping, assessment, etc.).
Stick Pick Link: stickpickapp.blogspot.com	
Team Shake Link: dontditchtech.com/teamshake	Sort students into groups.
Class Dojo Link: classdojo.com	Break students into groups easily.
Team Split Link: dontditchtech.com/teamsplit	Time various students or parties simultaneously (ninety-nine cents on Apple Store or Google Play).

MEANINGFUL

The principle "Meaningful" expresses that content instruction is designed and delivered with the students at the heart of all decisions and now becomes our central focus.

For many teachers, accounting for individual needs in the classroom is already extremely frustrating. It takes time. With a lack of available resources and little time for one-on-one instruction, creating meaningful content might seem like a tall order. But with planning, it's possible. In fact, you are probably doing a few things right already.

What are some signs that you are creating meaningful content? Ask yourself:

- Do you account for student interests in content selection, or allow students to choose from a few options?

- Do you take student fluency, syntax, and reading ability into account when creating a lesson?

- Do you take student experiences (or lack thereof) into account, along with students' multiple linguistic, cultural, and familial backgrounds?

Let's look at how using tech can ease your stress around creating meaningful content. Joe Marquez, a K–12 education strategist for CDW-G from California, was a former middle school science teacher. He suggests a multi-faceted approach to annotating articles that helps students dive deeply into them.

Joe's "Hyper-Annotation" Lesson

Lesson Structure and Sequence

Concept: "Analyzing News Articles"

Take a deep dive into a central theme. (Here, it's human space exploration.) The teacher distributes three texts, annotated in different ways, to the students.

Anticipatory Set: Teacher activates prior knowledge about the topic. A discussion about the SpaceX launch could yield discussion about prior rocket launches, products invented through the space program, etc. Students read the article. Together or separately, the teacher and students make ties from initial conversations to the topic to be discussed.

To prepare for digital transformation of the article, download a PDF of the article with NewsELA or the Mercury Reader Chrome extension and convert it to a Google Docs document.

For detailed instructions, go to
DitchThatTextbook.com/hyperannotate.

This lesson is differentiated in depth and complexity.

Differentiation

Group One: Students add two columns next to the article— one for thoughts and comments and one for images. They add to those columns right next to the corresponding text in the article.

Bloom's taxonomy: Understand

Group Two: Students create two columns as Group One did. They also use the Highlight Tool add-on in Google Docs to highlight different parts of the article (i.e., historical information, description of launch day, specifications of the rocket, etc.). Highlight Tool gathers and sorts highlighted text at the end of the document.

Bloom's taxonomy: Analyze and distinguish

Group Three: Students will complete Group Two's activities and will add one of the following choice activities:

- Add a student-created image or diagram with Google Drawings.
- Hyperlink outside resources and add sticky notes with the "Note Anywhere" Chrome extension.

Bloom's taxonomy: Evaluate and justify decisions

The differentiated groups of the same article come together to discuss what they learned from the reading. They can do this face-to-face with a student taking notes. See the one-pager template and make your own copy of it at DitchThatTextbook. com/onepager.

Through this discussion, students identify the three main ideas gleaned from the article.

As a group, the students create a presentation with each student given a role. This can be the role to complete a single slide, add the text, find the images, or create diagrams.

Once completed, the groups get together with groups who completed the same tasks for the other two assigned articles. Each group presents their findings while recording a screencast of their presentation. Students can also present to peers as an interactive slide deck with tools like Nearpod (nearpod.com) or Pear Deck (peardeck.com).

These presentations are then uploaded to Flipgrid so that other students may view and comment on the group presentations.

How to Get Started with Meaningful Differentiation

- Consider how content can be individualized based on students' interests and choices. Can student choice be embedded in your lessons?
- Consider fluency, syntax, and reading ability in your lesson content. Create or alter accordingly (See the previous section on intentionality.).
- Embed students' cultural, familial, and community backgrounds into content choices.

Extensions and Other Applications for Meaningful Differentiation:

Instructional Technology	How to Use this App
Insert Learning Link: insertlearning.com	Turn any website into an interactive and varied learning experience.
T Smithsonian Reader Link: tweentribune.com	Provide materials as varied reading levels.
Dogo News Link: dogonews.com	
NewsELA Link: newsela.com	
Google News Archives Link: news.google.com/newspapers	Introduce historical and current newspapers from around the world.
Google Arts and Culture Link: artsandculture.google.com	Open a portal to images and experiences that represent students' varied backgrounds and interests.
NASA Wavelength Link: nasawavelength.org	Provide a collection of content on earth-space science.
Wonderopolis Link: wonderopolis.org	Encourage "wonderings" based on promoting a sense of curiosity. Content levels vary.
NumberNut Link: numbernut.com	Engage students in varied levels of math content.
ExploreLearning Gizmos Link: explorelearning.com	Provide a treasure trove of varied math and science simulations (free simulations with an account that changes weekly and paid version also available).
News-O-Matic Link: newsomatic.org	Explore current events "newspaper" offered at multiple levels in multiple languages just for kids.

Variety

The principle "variety" means opening access to multiple teacher-curated or other expert-created content areas for learners based on their preferences. "Variety is the spice of life" also applies to learning. So consider how you can vary the way your content is taught so as to engage varied students.

(For further review of the heart of this concept, check out CAST organization's tremendously important work around the framework of Universal Design for Learning (UDL) at cast.org. CAST's and UDL's mission is to educate individuals on varied ways to engage with, represent, and express their content knowledge.)

You might ask yourself questions related to Variety that determine if you are opening content access to meet student needs:

- Do I display information for auditory, visual, and kinesthetic preferences?

- Is support provided to decode symbols and academic language? (This might overlap with linguistic support.)

- Are ways included to organize content, highlight important points, and promote transfer of knowledge?

Kara Heichelbech, an instructional technology coach from the Indianapolis, Indiana, area, provided this lesson that she teaches in her business and technology courses.

KARA'S ABBREVIATED MARKETING LESSON: (ANTICIPATING AND REHEARSAL)

LESSON STRUCTURE AND SEQUENCE

Concept: "Marketing Mix"

Identify the 4 Ps of the marketing mix.

Anticipatory Set: Teacher will bring in different, familiar products and ask students' knowledge of the products (e.g., Tide, Nike shoes, Doritos or Cheetos, etc.).

Differentiated rehearsal and elaboration can be based on group (color-coded) assignment group. See orange column.

DIFFERENTIATION

Group One: Students will apply vocabulary (price, product, place, promotion) on a Padlet using the teacher's examples as well as recall from the class discussion.

Bloom's taxonomy: Recall or write

Group Two: Students will identify the 4 Ps of three similar products of their choice. Using their research skills, students will identify not only the initial, basic 4 Ps but also a deeper understanding of the vocabulary. An example can be found at dontditchtech.com/marketing.

Bloom's taxonomy: Restate in own words

Group three: Allowing for choice, students will identify and create their own Ps for either a product that needs revamping or a new product. Students can use a variety of mediums to demonstrate their knowledge of a product's 4 Ps, such as Canva, Adobe Spark, Smore, Padlet, or even a video, podcast, or blog.

Bloom's taxonomy: Apply content in different context

How to Get Started with Variety for Differentiation

- Analyze how content is shared with learners. Are there visual, auditory, and kinesthetic means of sharing content with learners, at least across a few lessons within a unit?

- Are there chances for students to decode symbols and academic language?

- Ensure that strategies for organizing content and highlighting the most important points are shared with students. Is the transfer of knowledge promoted in your lesson?

Extensions and Other Applications for Variety in Differentiation

Instructional Technology	How to Use this App
Google Classroom Link: classroom.google.com	Act as landing spaces that allow you to offer multiple means of learning content.
HyperDocs and HyperSlides Link: docs.google.com/about Link: google.com/slides/about	
Thinglink Link: thinglink.com	
VoiceThread Link: voicethread.com	Teach material in both auditory and visual fashion with opportunities to gauge learning.
Edpuzzle Link: edpuzzle.com	
Desmos.com Link: desmos.com	Have a more powerful graphing calculator.

Instructional Technology	How to Use this App
Iorad Link: iorad.com	Create step-by-step tutorials easily, especially helpful for procedural knowledge.
Newspaper Map Link: newspapermap.com	Offer timely newspaper accounts from around the world in multiple languages.
Newseum Link: newseum.org	
Khan Academy Link: khanacademy.org	Act as an online portal for lessons in math, computers, economics, science, history and more.
NBC Learn Link: nbclearn.com	Act as a collection of original source videos for grades K–12+.
GoNoodle Link: gonoodle.com	Act as a site for embedding movement in your classroom.
Natural Reader Link: naturalreaders.com	Act as a professional text-to-speech program that converts any written text into spoken words.
Global Voices Link: globalvoices.org	Act as a current events newspaper in multiple languages.

IMPROVING STUDENT PRODUCT

N ow that we have moved our roles along the continuum of the foundational elements of differentiation and actual lesson design, let's start to think about how we differentiate for students to optimize their abilities in sharing what they know.

This chapter will not have examples for all five specific categories (from Pilot to Creative Art Coach) but will instead integrate Museum Exhibitor, Restaurant Owner, and Councilmember into one. The narrowing of roles happens because we know that all strong lessons have both formative and summative assessment opportunities. The differences inherent in these three roles, at least under the lens of assessment, are miniscule. At the end of the day, we have to gather data from both formative and summative assessments to gauge student learning and to evaluate our teaching.

What varies is how we allow students to express their knowledge and skills. Our focus in this chapter is how students can best show what they know in differentiated ways using technology.

When used purposefully, tech assists us in monitoring learning and provides students with a greater variety of ability-sharing than do paper and pencil tasks. Consider this: If someone were to ask you to best (and most easily) express what you know about your teaching area, how would you prefer to communicate your knowledge and skills? Writing? Speech? Movement? Students, just like teachers, have their own preferences and tendencies. As you begin your journey toward the integration of technology to differentiate, think about varied mechanisms for how students best show what they know. You might consider a voice recording or a written expression of knowledge; for example, let's say the instructional objective is to apply vocabulary in an explanation. Both an oral expression and written form can gauge application, so differentiation would mean that students could choose either form of expression—a voice recording or an online journal. Remember, what they know should circle back to your instructional objective(s) no matter how they show it.

Again, as the roles on our original chart progress, so can the diversity of student thinking, creativity, and technological apps. Challenge yourself to dip your toe in and eventually start swimming!

Pilot

Because the role of Pilots will typically use technology unidirectionally from teacher to student, assessments will often look like controlled prompts or leveled questions. Pilots, however, can still find a wide variety of destinations they'd like their students to reach, even if it's all to the same place. Let's check out a few.

Socrative (socrative.com)

Pilots can use Socrative for engaging portions of lessons or on-the-fly assessments. There are quizzes, space races, and other interactive options. And it gathers and stores your data.

Telestory (dontditchtech.com/telestory)

Telestory is a mobile app that guides students through the visual storytelling process. It provides prompts to help students write and record and even provides a fun frame and prop overlays. Students can save their video creations to the camera roll of their mobile device and share it from there.

Educreations (educreations.com)

Educreations provides a platform for whiteboard recording. Using an iPad, students can start a recording and draw on the screen, describing a process, explaining a concept, or retelling events they've read about. Students can use Educreations to describe their process for solving problems in math and science, which displays their thinking.

AnswerGarden (answergarden.ch)

Help students create something together with a single word or phrase. Answer Garden collects student responses to a single question and shapes them into a word cloud. The most common responses are displayed larger than less common responses. In this way, students can work together digitally to create a work of word art.

GradeCam (gradecam.com)

GradeCam can be used with any teacher-created prompt or problem, and a teacher's camera, phone, or computer can scan students' responses off printed sheets. (Think modern-day Scantron.)

ClassTools (classtools.net)

ClassTools has either a random name and topic-selection device, used together or separately. It's great for teachers who are mobile or who want to choose random students to answer assessment prompts. It's the *nouveau* way to draw sticks or names.

Vocaroo (vocaroo.com)

Vocaroo allows you to create a link to verbal and auditory feedback on your students' visual art, projects, or written work. If your students don't have a personal device, the link can be embedded in your school LMS. It is easy to use, and even the graduate students appreciate the personalized feedback.

Museum Exhibitor, Restaurant Owner, and Councilmember

 Here the teacher provides limited options, and students do not have full input on the broadest ranges of ways to express their knowledge. Nonetheless,

across a variety of apps and opportunities within a unit of study, students can differ in the ways they express their knowledge. Let's look at a few suggestions for Museum Exhibitors, Restaurant Owners, and Councilmembers.

Google Slides or Drawings
(slides.google.com or drawings.google.com)

Slides and Drawings are two versatile G Suite tools with applications far beyond oral reports in front of class. Create an icon board, making available various icons, images, lines, arrows, shapes, and text boxes for students to use. Students can copy and drag those items on a slide and create a quick infographic. This demonstrates what they know with creative words and images that bring their impressions into assessment, and they don't have to start from scratch.

NATE'S TIP

Check out this example of a graphic organizer activity I've done with students in my class. One thing that really helps this activity work is to create a template that students can copy and modify. Normally, when you share a document with students, they have to either go make a copy themselves, or they accidentally edit your master copy. No more! Instead, when you give them the share link, make a small change to the URL:

- Look for the word "edit" in the URL (It will be toward the right.).
- Replace "edit" with the word "copy."
- Now, when students use the URL, it will automatically prompt them to make a new copy.

Nate's Example: dontditchtech.com/organizer

BUNCEE (BUNCEE.COM)

Buncee is a design platform built for the classroom. Students can choose or add their own images and animations to accompany text describing what they've learned. Bonus: Buncee creations are highly shareable.

CREATIVE ART COACH

At this level of differentiation, the teacher might set evaluative criteria or even work jointly with students to do so, but the heart of differentiating outcomes in this role is that students use technology to create their own unique ways of expressing their knowledge. So choice and variety are at the center of these technologies used to create student product. Let's take a look at a few apps and opportunities for Creative Art Coaches.

STORYBIRD (STORYBIRD.COM)

StoryBird is visual storytelling for everyone. Students can express their knowledge and understanding through the creation of a story bird. It's visual creativity at its best.

TRELLO (TRELLO.COM)

Trello is a platform for creating boards to share information, knowledge, media, and lists. The boards are displayed for the teacher in an easy-to-read format and work well for managing group projects.

ANGIE'S ADVICE

Often, students are already familiar and comfortable with certain apps and websites. They might have filled their digital toolboxes with tools and are ready to go. Others might have individual tools that they love that you don't know about. With student choice, have students describe their vision for their projects to you and check in regularly to make sure their projects meet your academic needs.

IMOVIE

A solid video-editing tool included on iPhones and other Apple products is iMovie. When students want to demonstrate their full creative capacities to show off what they know, iMovie lets them flourish. Bring video clips—along with images, text overlays, and more—into this powerful editor. Pre-made templates can be used to create movie trailer-style videos (a popular classroom option), short TED Talk-style presentations, explainer videos, and more. Let students level up their skills with even more sophisticated tools, such as Camtasia (techsmith.com/video-editor.html) or Final Cut Pro (apple.com/final-cut-pro) (for Apple products only).

SKETCHNOTES

Sketchnotes let students mix verbal and visual learning in one custom image. Even your less artistic students can thrive here with stick figures and simple doodles. (Sketchnote expert Mike Rohde says almost any object can be drawn with a combination of five elements: squares, triangles, circles, lines, and dots. Try it!) Digital sketchnoting has its advantages, including the undo button and unlimited colors, and works best on tablets or touchscreens. Paper sketches, however, can provide a tactile experience some students will love. Check out tablet apps, such as Paper by WeTransfer (paper.bywetransfer.com), Adobe Draw (adobe.com/products/draw.html), or Procreate (procreate.art/ipad).

Google Drawings (drawings.google.com)

Google Drawings is a great visual creation tool in G Suite. It's an alternative to sketchnotes for laptops or Chromebooks or if you want students to have more control than the icon boards above allow. Combine text and shapes with icons from a source like the Noun Project (thenounproject.com) or Flat Icon (flaticon.com) to make a brain-friendly link: DitchThatTextbook.com/infographics.

Rocketbooks (getrocketbook.com)

Used like a regular paper notebook, Rocketbooks can be the last notebooks you buy. The less expensive version is for one-time use, but with the scan of your phone, all of your students' handwritten notes are sent to the Rocketbook app and cloud.

Rocketbooks are a Creative Art Coach's dream. Imagine that you present students with a task or problem. Then together, you brainstorm a few different topics in which to develop their ideas or gather additional research, assigning each topic one Rocketbook icon. (Specific icons in a Rocketbook are saved to specific places in Google Drive, in this case.) Over time, your students will have created a library of research and thinking that they can "draw from," pun intended. Check out these recommendations from the site *Cult of Pedagogy* as a place to start: cultofpedagogy.com/note-taking.

MATT'S TIP

Giving students freedom to create can be empowering for them. But believe it or not, it can also be crippling. Giving them a "Go create whatever you want!" assignment can cause academic paralysis as they might think, "I don't even know where to start!" Gradually release freedom to students over time, guiding them as they learn how to use it. Provide extra freedom to students who will thrive with it—even if their products will look much different from everyone else's.

TEACHING WITH TRANSPARENCY

The previous chapters have given you many ideas on how to implement practical strategies and applications to better differentiate your classroom. In this next chapter, however, we're going to take a moment to step back and reconsider how those actions align with our philosophy toward our students and our school communities. Although we'll be discussing three quite seemingly disparate areas both inside and outside the classroom, you'll notice a common narrative that weaves between the threads: access and visibility.

Access & Visibility

#1. Transparent, Quality Models for Students and Parents

As we're sure you're aware, modeling is not exactly a new idea in education. The "I Do, We Do, You Do" model (or variations of it), proposed by Vygotsky in 1978 and Pearson and Gallagher in 1983, is used by teachers all the time. However, our push to differentiate the classroom through technology presents a unique opportunity of which teachers can and should take advantage.

More than has ever been possible before, teachers can distribute quality, accessible models of thinking, expectations, processes, and products to students and their families.

Nate recalls this anecdote from his classroom. One night, while posting on Flipgrid, one of my students—equipped with a Chromebook—had some sort of issue posting his video. His solution to the problem was to download a separate video recorder app, use another app to convert and submit it in the proper format, upload it to Google Drive, and then use a Google Form to turn it in separately. When I asked the student the next day how he knew to work through the solution and find another process to use, he gave me a one-word answer: "YouTube."

In that scenario, the student was lucky enough to find a quality model that showed him how to do each step and described how to avoid the numerous pitfalls that might have occurred along the way. But what might have happened if there were no good model to be found?

MATT'S NOTE

By giving models of our thinking, expectations, and processes to parents, we enable and equip them to serve as even better resources for their children. Clear guidelines allow teachers and parents or guardians to act as equal partners in the student's educational journey.

Technology now gives us the ability to provide reliable, comprehensive, and in-depth modeling to both students and their parents or guardians. If differentiation means that our classrooms become more varied, intentional, and meaningful as we suggested in Chapter H, then our modeling should be too.

Let's take a look at an example of this kind of modeling in action:

In his DCUSH course, Nate has his students create a choose-your-own-journey game. Nate takes students through each step of the process and provides copious resources and materials. What we'd like you to pay attention to, however, are the models and modeling that he provides for students and parents. Check out his resources by going to the following site or scanning the QR Codes:

Student Resources:
dontditchtech.com/studentcrush

Nate's Modeling:
dontditchtech.com/angiecalendar

Note: If you're looking to make choose-your-own-journey stories, we recommend checking out how to do this through Google Slides in Chapter C.

In his classroom (and with the help of an LMS, Canvas), students have access to these models at any time (even beforehand) as do their parents.

NATE'S NOTE

I didn't build this kind of classroom overnight, and neither should you. Start slowly by trying a few strategies at a time. Build your transparent classroom from there.

What are some things that you can do to start opening your modeling to students and parents?

- Model the product that you want students to create as well as the thinking and skills you would like them to use.

- Create a Screencast (Screencastify, Screencast-O-Matic, or QuickTime) that demonstrates how to do one activity from class and the thinking you expect to see.

- Test out making a digital tutorial on iorad to share with students and parents. (See more on how to use iorad in Chapter I².)

- Highlight both teacher and prior student models of work and compare and contrast the two.

- Make a class Twitter chat or hashtag that provides models and hints for challenging pieces of homework.

- Create intermittent check points, especially at the mid-point of larger projects.

#2. Making Content, Skills, and Yourself Available

The filing cabinet was once a teacher's reliable go-to for activities, worksheets, or review packets. Students' lived experiences and skills, however, have surpassed the stagnant tools found in filing cabinets. Without exaggerating, a student today in the span of thirty minutes can:

1. Order a custom pizza using an emoji.
2. Snapchat a few friends to come over and enjoy it with them.

3. Fix their bike while they're waiting with help from a YouTube tutorial.

4. And post a few pics on Instagram once the pizza has arrived.

As educators, we are thus left with a question: Does our teaching inside our classrooms reflect the way students learn outside of them? It should! Because when we make the learning in our classroom more accessible to our children, we:

- Allow students more flexibility to learn in terms of time (ahead of schedule, behind schedule, as review, visual for language support, etc.).

- Equip students' families with the same content and skill knowledge, allowing them to become more involved in their child's day-to-day schooling.

- Position teachers as more positive, accurate, and meaningful resources for students.

- Better meet the needs of students who need additional exposure to skills and content, such as students who:

  » have Individualized Education Plans (IEPs)

  » are English Language Learners (ELLs)

  » are dealing with extenuating circumstances, such as prolonged absences, moving to/from another school, etc.

To keep up with our students' lived experiences in the twenty-first century, we as educators need to adapt the way that we make our own skills and content available to them.

What can you do to start opening up access to your classroom's content and skills?

- Consider adding more access to your lessons, activities, and other resources via your school's LMS if you have one.

ANGIE'S ADVICE

Remember, you don't have to have an LMS like Canvas to distribute materials, models, and other resources to students. A well-organized Google Drive that uses shared HyperDocs or HyperSlides can be just as effective.

- Share a basic calendar of weekly or daily events with parents and students alike. You can easily build or share one in Google Docs or Google Sheets or print them out to be taken home. If you'd like a sample of one Nate created for his classroom, go to: dontditchtech.com/natecalendar.

  Note: His calendar is a bit more complex since he teaches high school; you can tailor your calendar to your own appropriate level of depth.). Additionally, Angie has a shortened college course calendar here: dontditchtech.com/angiecalendar with Google links embedded. She is moving toward linking every formal assessment to a sample or a portion of a sample. Remember, if you're looking for models, former students are often willing to show off to your new classes!

- Give students a preview of upcoming work through teasers on Twitter or Instagram. The more cliffhanger-ish, the better. Check out the hashtag #qiinhistory (quite interesting in history) on Twitter for some of Nate's own examples.

- Share access to rubrics and grading practices through an app like Google Drive, Google Sites, ThingLink, or LiveBinders. Or consider coaching students how to create their own assessment criteria.

- For an advanced strategy, try creating a YouTube channel and upload screencasts. Quite a few steps are involved in the process, but with a basic screencasting app and a YouTube profile, you can create and share content. If you'd like help on starting an educator page, check out YouTube itself or reach out to us on Twitter @teachfromridge. You can see an example at youtube.com/ridgwayhistory.

Increasing access to the classroom isn't just limited to content and skills. We also need to address the way that teachers can meet the communication needs of twenty-first-century students and parents. In a world that is interconnected by the internet, teachers need to be as plugged in as their communities are. This means having more examples, expectations, and communications at your school community's fingertips.

What are some useful apps that can be used to increase and ease communication between yourself, parents, and students? Check out the charts below and think about which one of our favorite apps might work best for you.

Remind (remind.com)

- Cost: Free
- Purpose: Communication between teachers, students, and parents
- Features: Phone number anonymity, easy-to-use, can be used with non-smartphones

Edmodo (edmodo.com)

- Cost: Free
- Purpose: Classroom organization and communication

Simply Circle (simplycircle.com)

- Features: All-in-one service platform
- Cost: Free, but only for one teacher and twenty students and parents total, then $4.99 per month
- Purpose: Classroom organization and communication
- Features: Great for elementary classrooms and used for family engagement

Bloomz (bloomz.net)

- Cost: Free
- Purpose: Classroom organization and communication
- Features: Includes sections for other school affiliates, such as PTA, etc.

Class Dojo (classdojo.com)

- Purpose: Behavior management
- Cost: Free
- Purpose: Behavior management
- Features: Useful for Positive Behavioral Intervention and Supports (PBIS), fun and easy to use, and student friendly

#3. Showing It Off

If something amazing happens in your classroom, and no one knows about it, did it really ever happen?

The question above was posed at a keynote Nate and Angie attended in the summer of 2018 by education speaker and author

Kevin Honeycutt. At first, we weren't sure how to respond. This twist on the old philosophical question, "If a tree falls in the forest and no one is around, did it make a sound?" pushed us to meditate on our relationships with students and their families and the public perception of our jobs as educators.

Before we continue, ask yourself a couple of questions:

- What digital presence or footprint does your classroom have?

- Do your administrators, students' families, and the community know what is going on in your classroom?

Opening your classroom to the outside world provides you with the potential to produce dynamic results—for you, your students, and the world of education. Let's explore why.

Showing Off

For all that can be said about differentiation in the classroom, it's important to recognize that sharing their work with the world matters too. For example, let's take a look at Mrs. Wilson's project-based learning (PBL) unit:

PBL Unit: The Water Cycle and Sanitation Systems

- **Objective:** Demonstrate how the water cycle and sanitation systems work together to distribute and clean our water.

- **Task:** Propose solutions to poor drainage on the school playground.

- **Audience:** They can be peers, team teachers, and local engineering and sanitation companies via Skype or Google Hangouts.

Notice that the audience in this case refers a lot to what we discussed earlier about authenticity. Openness can play an instrumental part in meeting students' needs, such as their sources of support and feedback, their expectations of themselves, and ultimately, what they learn. Tech makes this more possible than ever before.

NATE'S NOTE

Does differentiation really play a part in opening your classroom to a real-world audience? Absolutely.

Remember, it can help students who need:
- more feedback and support,
- extra engagement, and
- higher levels of rigor. (Students who are gifted and talented need differentiated content too!)

Aside from improved learning opportunities, showing what students are learning has an added benefit of revealing us (educators) as the superheroes that we truly are—no bragging required! In our example above, Ms. Wilson's students, their families, her fellow staff members, and her administrators can all equally rejoice in the fact that they have a wonderful teacher in their midst.

Here's the reality: Twenty-first century teaching is tough. We educate children on everything from social skills to the vocabulary of nuclear reactions, yet a combination of poor perception, politics, and more has left educators embattled and our profession under siege. Think back to the question that opened this chapter: If something amazing happens in your classroom, and no one knows about it, did it really ever happen? Maybe the answer is another question. How can we expect the perceptions and policies surrounding education to change if our educational practices—digitally or otherwise—go unseen?

For every successful amazing activity and spark ignited in a child, we should show off our awesomeness and keep doing so. Transparency can mean a better world for all of us involved in our students' lives. One tweet, phone call, or digital portfolio sent to our school's families and communities can change the way your students' great learning is promoted!

How could you use technology to show off your students and your teaching to the world? Remember, it can start small with a simple phone call or email home.

TWITTER (TWITTER.COM)

You might think that Twitter is just for news organizations or celebrities—and you're right! Don't forget, you **are** a celebrity with news to share. Setting up a Twitter profile only takes a few minutes and creating a hashtag about your room takes even less time. For more on Twitter and how to use it, check out our blurb on Twitter in Chapter I[1].

SEESAW (WEB.SEESAW.ME)

SeeSaw is an online digital portfolio app that can be shared among all school stakeholders. What makes it especially powerful is that all parties (teachers, parents, and students) can examine growth in real time and longitudinally. Check out this video to see how this was done in one primary school classroom: dontditchtech.com/seesaw.

FLIPGRID (FLIPGRID.COM)

We've already mentioned several ways that Flipgrid can be used in the classroom. But did you know it can also connect you with other educators and larger learning communities around the globe? For more on how to take Flipgrid outside your own school's walls, check out the Disco Library tab under your Flipgrid Profile.

TEACHING KIDS TO REFLECT

W e want students to be thinkers, to be able to pursue a topic deeply from many angles, and to come to a useful conclusion about it. But how do they become better at that thinking? By thinking about how they think. When students (or any of person, for that matter) can understand what kind of thinkers they are, they can also take steps to make themselves better thinkers.

That's metacognition—thinking about thinking. And the results can unlock learning in powerful ways, context-free! In this final chapter, we're going to examine how to use technology to develop students' metacognitive practices.

Regardless of how or whether we integrate tech, empowering students to develop as thinkers means that they will eventually begin to carry the cognitive load in the classroom. Metacognition is a different skill than critical thinking. And like any skill, it has to be developed. Researchers Wolfgang Schneider and Michael Pressley, in their work "Memory Development Between 2 and 20," note that students equipped with metacognitive knowledge about reading and memory improve their use of learning strategies. In their studies, they found that metacognition gave students the capacity to understand when and why they should use certain learning approaches. If we want students to own their learning as they grow and develop, metacognition is a must.

Being metacognitively aware, especially with the help of technology, also allows twenty-first-century learners to have confidence in sorting the millions of pieces of new information they are likely to encounter even within any given school year. With such reflective power, learners not only begin to develop a sense of how they learn and remember, but they also learn to discard less important information and study more effectively.

In a classroom where metacognitive processes are taught and enacted, the atmosphere will begin to feel more like a Creative Art Coach's studio than a Pilot's cockpit. Students will use their new knowledge of how they best learn and remember to express preferences for how they learn and are assessed. When teachers know what students' learning preferences are, this can help us design lessons accordingly.

How can instructional technology help in developing metacognitive processes and student reflection? Let's look at a few specific areas and discuss some practical strategies where technology can make the cognitive load easier to lift and students more effective in their learning.

Area #1: Goal Setting

With or without technology in our classrooms, there are often distractions. Teaching in the 1990s meant intercom announcements, students knocking at your door, or colleagues dropping off messages. Today, teachers deal with smartphones buzzing, smartwatches dinging, or endless email notifications. Nonetheless, we have to create good flow in our classrooms as defined by Mihaly Csikszentmihalyi. One of the key elements of flow, according to Csikszentmihalyi, is goal-setting. Instructional technology is a brilliant way to create goals, house them, and tie the knot in promoting student reflection on predetermined goals.

The following apps can help teachers model types of goals to be set, create prompts, and gather goals in one central place for review. Eventually, learners view large learning tasks and begin to create goals for themselves. Instructional technology allows students to return to their goals in the final step: reflection.

Google Forms (google.com/forms/about)

Google Forms is an easy form creator platform that can house qualitative and quantitative data. Responses can be compiled into a Google Sheet.

> **Idea for use:** Create a form for measuring goals. Have students create a simple one themselves or have them copy one you've created. Have them fill in text fields, "Where I'm progressing?" or "What I need help with?" or "Big wins for the week." Have students respond to the prompts in their forms periodically (twice weekly, weekly, every two weeks, etc.) and review data in the spreadsheet.

ONE NOTE (ONENOTE.COM/DOWNLOAD)

One Note is a great app for older students to record thoughts, ideas, and to-dos in one space.

> **Idea for use:** Create a goal journal. Students can add entries to it periodically. *Tip:* Have students add new entries at the top of the page instead of the bottom for reverse chronological order.

PADLET (PADLET.COM)

With Padlet, you can create a prompt via a web-based bulletin board for ideas and collaboration. Students only need to click and type, but they can also add rich multimedia notes with images, videos, audio, and more.

> **Note:** This is a "freemium" site with a free version and a paid premium version. Students can create a free account and use one of their free Padlet boards for this activity.

> **Ideas for use:** Create a learning gallery with exhibits that demonstrate progress toward goals. Add images, text, links, voice recordings, and more. Create a "home base" for student Padlet "learning galleries" with links to each student's Padlet board. This creates community and lets students see one another's progress.

Angie uses Padlet as a quick brainstorm (and pre-assessment) in her graduate "Adolescent Development" class when she asks students to reflect on prior teaching experiences. See her example here: dontditchtech.com/padlet.

ANSWER GARDEN (ANSWERGARDEN.CH)

Students generate short responses based on a prompt. Students only need to click and type.

> **Idea for use:** Students can respond to a short prompt, describing what portion or steps of a project they have completed (e.g., listing steps 1–2 complete, or 50 percent complete, leaving the teacher with a transcript of the entire class's completion rate). The exercise in itself prompts students to review their progress.

Angie used Answer Garden in an undergraduate course to track how much school-based field participation teacher candidates had completed. This semester, she added an example here of how a brainstorm was conducted on Answer Garden. This brainstorm led to a reflective exercise on how to connect a field-based experience with academic vocabulary. It makes a great substitute if Twitter is blocked in your classroom or school. See an example here: dontditchtech.com/ag.

GOOGLE CALENDAR (GOOGLE.COM/CALENDAR/ABOUT)

Google Calendar is a web-based calendar where groups can share due dates, set up video Hangouts, and input deadlines.

MY STUDY LIFE (MYSTUDYLIFE.COM)

My Study Life organizes classes, tasks, and projects in one app.

> **Idea for use:** With Google Calendar or My Study Life, students can set mile marker goals, intermediate goals that show progress like mile markers do on the highway. Students log these intermediate goals as events. If they don't reach them,

it prompts the discussion as to why. Was the goal unrealistic? Was the work more time-intensive than expected? Students can reset the mile markers if necessary.

Area #2: Chunking

Because learners often have access to very large amounts of content, we need to guide them in determining what is most important or how to categorize information. In 1956, George Miller of Harvard published a paper in *Psychological Review* titled "The Magical Number Seven, Plus or Minus Two: Some Limits on Our Capacity for Processing Information." Miller's work resulted from a series of cognitive load experiments he and others created. The results determined that individuals could successfully hold five to seven pieces of information.

Given that most experts estimate that we see more than one hundred times more information in a day today when compared with fifty years ago, we need to help students chunk or organize content. Otherwise, they are simply on cognitive overload.

These apps help learners break large amounts of declarative knowledge into categories, procedural knowledge into manageable steps, and eventually teach learners to create these chunks themselves. Remember, you want to shift away from flying that learning vessel yourself into teaching your students to be the Pilots of their own journeys.

MindMup (mindmup.com)

MindMup is an easy-to-use mind-mapping software.

> **Idea for use:** Map it out. Students can start with a main idea at the middle of a MindMup map. Branch out that main idea into the parts that make it up, then branch again (and again,

if necessary). A traditional semantic map has great benefits, and MindMups are easy to share with others and recall later.

GOOGLE SHEETS (GOOGLE.COM/SHEETS/ABOUT)

Google Sheets is a sheet creator that can be collaborative.

Idea for use: Let conditional formatting do some initial chunking for you. Create rules that automatically change the color of cells based on the information in them by going to Format -> Conditional Formatting. For example, if your data is numbers, create a rule that automatically changes the color to a darker shade of red as the number rises. If data is words, highlight cells a certain color if they have a certain word. For a video tutorial on setting up conditional formatting, go to dontditchtech.com/conditional.

TRELLO (TRELLO.COM/TOUR)

Trello creates boards, lists, and cards for project management.

Idea for use: Trello lets you create lists of lists, which is great for breaking down big ideas and projects into manageable chunks. Students can add cards with images, text, and labels to lists. The slick part of Trello for the teacher is that many student entries can be viewed on a single page.

THINGLINK (THINGLINK.COM/EDU)

With Thinglink, you can embed live links (texts, pics, or video) into a document or onto a visual, such as a PDF for sorting, chunking, and organizing.

Idea for use: Create a collage of images with an image editing tool like Canva or Google Drawings. Students can upload the collage to Thinglink and add clickable hotspots to the collage. This helps students break a big idea into smaller sections (the collage) and see details in each section (the clickable hotspots).

Area #3: Problem Solving for Self-Regulation

As we create community with the students who arrive at our doors from varied backgrounds and sometimes strife, we occasionally see that the culture of immediate gratification causes issues in our classrooms.

In her book, *Fall Down 7 Times, Get Up 8*, Debbie Silver suggests that adults model the thinking and behavior that they want to see in children. She recommends, "Adults can help students learn to internalize self-regulation by modeling the behavior they want to see in children. Orally elaborating (thinking aloud) about one's choice emphasizes the conscious nature of taking control of the situation." In other words, turn the productive thinking and actions over to the learners themselves.

Silver suggests we teach students to "stop and think" and follow a problem-solving strategy. So how can technology help in this particular area of reflective practice? Two possibilities emerge. The first is finding a prompt that teases out the way students are feeling and experiencing the world. The second is having a shared space where reflective, self-regulatory thoughts can be processed and potentially shared.

Consider the following apps for such activities. They provide content and mechanisms for working with a range of ages from littles to adolescent learners.

Sesame Street's "Breathe, Think, and Do" (sesamestreet.org)

Ideas for use: "Breathe, Think, and Do" not only provides real-life examples of situations that tax children emotionally but also offers small children steps for solving problems. It can be launched via a tablet, iPad, or computer and targeted for particular areas where children struggle.

Teachers can use "Breathe, Think, and Do" to set up discussions with students, create role-play scenarios, and provide support for situations that need emotional and social processing, such as handling separation anxiety, turn-taking, and frustration.

Class Dojo (classdojo.com)

Ideas for Use: Class Dojo is a one-stop shop for classroom management needs. Teachers take attendance on Class Dojo, track participation, and report to families. Class Dojo not only includes areas of behavioral concerns, such as participation and working hard, but also social and emotional skills, including teamwork and helping others. The new student portfolio section provides a forum for more direct communication between learners and adults.

Emotionary (funnyfeelings.com)

Ideas for Use: Emotionary is a treasure chest of vocabulary, video examples, and books to assist students in developing emotional intelligence and managing their reactions. It helps students develop their language to express exactly how they are feeling and experiencing the world. And it is available in Spanish too. Teachers can use the materials from Emotionary to create reflective prompts that are later shared in a Google Form, Trello, Penzu, or another reflective journal format.

Middle School Confidential (middleschoolconfidential.com)

Ideas for use: Middle School Confidential is a series of graphic novels for grades six to nine and curricular materials that creatively tackle emotional struggles for early teens. Teachers can use the graphic novels, for example, to create reflective prompts that are later housed in a Google form, Trello, Penzu, or another reflective journal. Angie is using this series to teach future teachers to reflect upon the social and emotional development of early adolescence and to help them tackle these issues with their future learners.

Area #4: Evaluation and Reflection

The apps that follow will assist students as they evaluate their progress, contemplate varied approaches for learning content (more on this in Chapter H), and evaluate learning approaches and final products. Until your students develop the habit of reflective thinking, develop and model prompts for them.

Some examples might be:

- This topic was easy (or hard) to learn because____.

- What helped me learn ____ was ____.

- I can do better ____ if I ____.

- My teacher or classmates helped me learn ____ because____.

Or for secondary-level students:

- This topic was easy or challenging for me because____.

- What helped me to learn most easily was____.

- If I think about my learning, what I can do to learn more easily is____.

- Family and friends might support my learning by _____.

Google Forms (google.com/forms/about)

Ideas for use: The creation and launch of a Google Form can provide you with tremendous insight into student effort, self-perception, and progress. Since data can be displayed collectively or viewed by individual student response, Google Forms can allow a teacher to see data in an instant.

Here is a reflective form Angie created for her sophomore-level college course: dontditchtech.com/reflect

Penzu (penzu.com/aboutus)

Ideas for use: An online journal that can house student responses to prompts that promote metacognitive practice. Penzu has options for private notes and for sharing. Provide students with some of the questions above. They can create short responses in Penzu and go back to them later.

Flipgrid (flipgrid.com)

Ideas for use: Flipgrid lets students generate and record responses aimed at reflections on learning and studying. The heart of great reflection is in the prompted thinking and scaffolding that occurs. This format is ideal for providing a prompt and allowing students to reflect. Plus students can view one another's prompts and provide feedback as well, thus forming a natural scaffolding.

CONCLUSION

In an earlier chapter, we compared technology to a hammer. If you got a new hammer, you probably wouldn't ask yourself, "Okay, now what can I do with a hammer?" You'd add it to your toolbox and pull out only the best and most important tools for building the end product you had in mind. The most important part of this analogy is the finished product—what was created with the tools and materials at your disposal.

Likewise, when we use technology in the classroom, it's not about the tools. It's not about finding the flashy, fun, popular apps and forcing them into instruction. Much like in carpentry, it's all about the finished product. How does teaching and learning build toward something worth creating, something that will be useful to our students or make their lives better?

When we take our eyes off the prize, we can easily lose our way. But when we fix our eyes on that ultimate goal, we'll use whatever we find that helps us get there. In today's world, ignoring the power of technology is akin to taking the toolbox and tool belt from the carpenter. It drastically limits what he or she can create. Focusing on the technology before the learning is like crediting beautiful photography to the camera. In reality, it takes a skilled photographer with a keen eye and deft control to capture an image that stirs us.

When we use technology to transform and differentiate instruction, we have to remember that technology isn't what makes the difference; it's the teacher and the learners who are key in the learning. Learning happens in powerful ways with and without technology. If you've read this book and believed that the best and only way to teach is through technology, then we have seriously failed you. Our hope is that you have discovered ways to use technology to amplify learning. That's the true hallmark of today's tech-infused education.

With all these new tools and ideas in your toolbelt, what do you do next? Here's what we'd like you to remember:

- **Keep learning.** Educators around the world are constantly sharing their best work and discussing the craft of teaching online. We've found that one of the fastest ways to improve as an educator is to learn from others. Explore how social media (i.e., Twitter, Pinterest, Facebook, Instagram, etc.)—or, more importantly, the people sharing and connecting there—can help you to grow. Don't limit your learning to your technology skills. You're only as good as your pedagogy—the art, practice, and science of teaching.

- **Be willing to try something new.** A saying from the entrepreneurial world applies here: "Fail fast." The best way to learn from your mistakes is to make them. The fastest way to improve on them is to evaluate them right away and make corrections. Reflect. It's not a recipe for the greatest comfort, but it will definitely help transform teaching and learning in your classroom.

- **Take small steps.** If you recall, we used the phrase *poco a poco* throughout this book. It means "little by little" in Spanish, and it's the best way to start with something new—teaching with tech, differentiating, or trying different concepts. Don't set yourself up for failure by trying too much even if you might want to. Small steps help you grow sustainably. They keep your students from feeling overwhelmed. And small steps add up—often faster than you imagine!

- **Differentiation isn't about making a hundred versions of every assignment.** This is one of the biggest misconceptions about differentiating instruction. A little variation, a little choice, and a little personalization can go a long way. They help students feel as if your class and your lesson were made just for them. In addition, they keep you from breaking your back lesson planning and grading. And they keep everyone from getting in a rut!

- **Let yourself show through.** The ideas we've shared in this book aren't hard and fast protocols for how teaching must look. They're nothing more than ideas. You can use them exactly as we described them. That said, ideas are very much a reflection of who we are as people and as educators. Your version of these ideas might look a little—or a lot—differently from ours. Your best version might take one tiny sprig of inspiration from what you've seen here in a whole new direction. No matter the case, let yourself and your students shine through your instruction. Whether you know it or whether they say it, your students crave to know you. Don't hide your unique self from them in the way you teach.

- **Reach for the next level.** We talked about the progression from Pilot to Museum Exhibitor to Restaurant Owner to Councilmember to Creative Art Coach. Here's a reminder from the beginning of the book: We are not static beings. We don't stay on the same level forever. Reach for that next level. One of the joys of teaching is seeing your skills improve because it means your students reap the rewards. Challenge yourself to reach the next level for the sake of your students. You are their model.

We're proud of you for taking this step. So are your students, your students' future families, their future employers, and all the people they'll come in contact with during their lives. The playwright Tom Stoppard once said, "Words are sacred. They deserve respect. If you get the right ones, in the right order, you might nudge the world a little." Education is very much like this. Teach the right lessons in the right way, and you can nudge the world a little bit.

It's up to you. We know you can do it. We *need* you to do it.

Now go out there and change the world!

Much love,

Matt, Nate, and Angie

> TEACH THE RIGHT LESSONS IN THE RIGHT WAY, AND YOU CAN NUDGE THE WORLD A LITTLE BIT.

BIBLIOGRAPHY

Atkinson, R. C. and R. M. Shiffin. "Human Memory: A Proposed System and Its Control Processes." In *The Psychology of Learning and Motivation 2*, edited by K. W. Spence and J. T. Spence, 89-195. New York: Academic Press, 1968.

Classtime. Retrieved from classtime.com/en

Csikszentmihalyi, Mihaly. *Flow: The Psychology of Optimal Experience*. New York: Harper and Row, 1990.

Ladson-Billings, G. *The Dreamkeepers*. San Francisco: San Francisco: Jossey-Bass, 1994.

Miller, G. A. "The Magical Number Seven, Plus or Minus Two: Some Limits on our Capacity for Processing Information." *Psychological Review* 63, no. 2 (1956): 81–97.

Miller, M. *Ditch That Textbook: Free Your Teaching and Revolutionize Your Classroom*. San Diego: Dave Burgess Consulting, Inc, 2015.

"Chapter 1: Elementary and Secondary Mathematics and Science Education." *National Science Foundation: Science and Engineering Indicators 2018 (NSB-2018-1)*. January 2018. nsf. gov/statistics/2018/nsb20181/report/sections/elementary-and-secondary-mathematics-and-science-education/instructional-technology-and-digital-learning.

Pearson, P.D., and M. Gallagher. "The Instruction of Reading Comprehension." *Contemporary Educational Psychology* 8, no. 3 (1983): 317–344.

Pew Research (May 2018). Retrieved from pewinternet. org/2018/05/31/teens-social-media-technology-2018/

Schneider, W. and M. Pressley, M. *Memory Development between 2 and 20*. New York: Springer-Verlag, 1989.

Silver, D. *Fall Down 7 Times Get Up 8: Teaching Kids to Succeed.* Thousand Oaks: Corwin Press, 2012.

Stoppard, T. *The Real Thing.* New York: The Strand Theatre. November 16, 1982.

Tomlinson, C. A. and S. D. Allan. *Leadership for Differentiating Schools and Classrooms.* Alexandria: Association of Supervision and Curriculum Development, 2000.

Vygotzky, L. and M. Cole. *Mind In Society: The Development of Higher Psychological Processes* (1st ed.). Boston: Harvard College, 1978.

ACKNOWLEDGMENTS

MATT MILLER

To my wife, Melanie, and my kids, Cassie, Hallie and Joel, whom I love dearly: You unyieldingly support me during my crazy travel and unconventional hours to pursue my dreams.

To Dave and Shelley Burgess, whose support has measurably changed my life and helped me to help educators all over the world: Thank you.

To the educators who have believed in this DITCH revolution, who have bravely tried new ideas and considered new philosophies: I get out of bed every morning inspired to serve you.

To Nate and Angie Ridgway, who dreamed of a book that combined all of our unique interests and talents: I've learned so much from you.

And most importantly, to my Lord and Savior Jesus Christ: You are my source of life, inspiration, and any talent bestowed upon me.

NATE RIDGWAY

Writing a book isn't possible without a team. I would like to thank my awesome wife, Annie, and my dad, Brock, for their unyielding support and unending hours of Booker watching and feedback-giving, and for limitless cups of coffee.

A very special thanks also goes to my two co-authors: my mom, Angie, and Matt Miller. You both have served as guiding inspirations on how to look at and shape the world.

Also, thanks to Dave and Shelley Burgess, as well as the entire publishing and editing team, Erin Casey, Mariana Lenox, and your entire team! You made this book possible.

Angie Ridgway

Inspiration comes from many sources. Every day, when I begin a lesson, my students and their ambition to be creative, engaging, student-centered teachers inspire me. They pretend that being "Dr. Ridgway's pedagogical guinea pigs" on the hamster wheel of life is fun. I thank them for their confidence and their affirmations. For their passion toward all things teaching, I am grateful.

To my sons, Nate and Keegan: It has always been a privilege to be your mom and your first teacher. The fact that you are determined to "make a difference" (a mantra in our household) warms my heart. And to Brock, Annie, Booker, and Cheyenne, thanks for your endless hours of listening to me and Nate discuss our philosophies and practices related to teaching. This book would not have been possible without your love and support. #Teamridgway is our foundation.

And, to my parents, Chuck, Ginny, and Rae: I am so blessed to have lived everything education from literally the time I was born. My parents are such great role models of all the possibilities of great public school education. Thanks for being the best role models of not only public service, but also of family unity.

Matt Miller, you have been an outstanding mentor. Without your knowledge, energy, and enduring support, this book would not be possible! And, to the team at Dave Burgess Consulting, Inc., you make it all look so easy! I am grateful.

MORE FROM

DAVE BURGESS
Consulting, Inc.

Since 2012, DBCI has been publishing books that inspire and equip educators to be their best. For more information on our DBCI titles or to purchase bulk orders for your school, district, or book study, visit **DaveBurgessConsulting.com/DBCIBooks**.

More from the *Like a PIRATE*™ Series

Teach Like a PIRATE by Dave Burgess

Explore Like a Pirate by Michael Matera

Learn Like a Pirate by Paul Solarz

Play Like a Pirate by Quinn Rollins

Run Like a Pirate by Adam Welcome

Lead Like a PIRATE™ Series

Lead Like a PIRATE by Shelley Burgess and Beth Houf

Balance Like a Pirate by Jessica Cabeen, Jessica Johnson, and Sarah Johnson

Lead with Culture by Jay Billy

Lead with Literacy by Mandy Ellis

Lead beyond Your Title by Nili Bartley

Leadership & School Culture

Culturize by Jimmy Casas

Escaping the School Leader's Dunk Tank by Rebecca Coda and Rick Jetter

The Innovator's Mindset by George Couros

Kids Deserve It! by Todd Nesloney and Adam Welcome

Let Them Speak! by Rebecca Coda and Rick Jetter

Start. Right. Now. by Todd Whitaker, Jeffrey Zoul, and Jimmy Casas

Stop. Right. Now. by Jimmy Casas and Jeffrey Zoul Jetter

The Limitless School by Abe Hege and Adam Dovico

The Pepper Effect by Sean Gaillard

The Principled Principal by Jeffrey Zoul and Anthony McConnell

The Secret Solution by Todd Whitaker, Sam Miller, and Ryan Donlan

They Call Me "Mr. De" by Frank DeAngelis

Relentless by Hamish Brewer

Unmapped Potential by Julie Hasson and Missy Lennard

Your School Rocks by Ryan McLane and Eric Lowe

Technology & Tools

50 Things You Can Do with Google Classroom by Alice Keeler and Libbi Miller

50 Things to Go Further with Google Classroom by Alice Keeler and Libbi Miller

140 Twitter Tips for Educators by Brad Currie, Billy Krakower, and Scott Rocco

Code Breaker by Brian Aspinall

Creatively Productive by Lisa Johnson

Google Apps for Littles by Christine Pinto and Alice Keeler

Master the Media by Julie Smith

Shake Up Learning by Kasey Bell

Social LEADia by Jennifer Casa-Todd

Teaching Math with Google Apps by Alice Keeler and
  Diana Herrington

Teachingland by Amanda Fox and Mary Ellen Weeks

Teaching Methods & Materials

All 4s and 5s by Andrew Sharos

Ditch That Homework by Matt Miller and Alice Keeler

Ditch That Textbook by Matt Miller

EDrenaline Rush by John Meehan

Educated by Design by Michael Cohen

The EduProtocol Field Guide by Marlena Hebern and
  Jon Corippo

Instant Relevance by Denis Sheeran

LAUNCH by John Spencer and A.J. Juliani

Make Learning MAGICAL by Tisha Richmond

Pure Genius by Don Wettrick

Shift This! by Joy Kirr

Spark Learning by Ramsey Musallam

Sparks in the Dark by Travis Crowder and Todd Nesloney

Table Talk Math by John Stevens

The Classroom Chef by John Stevens and Matt Vaudrey

The Wild Card by Hope and Wade King

The Writing on the Classroom Wall by Steve Wyborney

Inspiration, Professional Growth, & Personal Development

Be REAL by Tara Martin

Be the One for Kids by Ryan Sheehy

The EduNinja Mindset by Jennifer Burdis

Empower Our Girls by Lynmara Colón and Adam Welcome

The Four O'Clock Faculty by Rich Czyz

How Much Water Do We Have? by Pete and Kris Nunweiler

P Is for Pirate by Dave and Shelley Burgess

The Path to Serendipity by Allyson Apsey

Through the Lens of Serendipity by Allyson Apsey

Sanctuaries by Dan Tricarico

Shattering the Perfect Teacher Myth by Aaron Hogan

Stories from Webb by Todd Nesloney

Talk to Me by Kim Bearden

The Zen Teacher by Dan Tricarico

Children's Books

Dolphins in Trees by Aaron Polansky

The Princes of Serendip by Allyson Apsey

BRING
DON'T DITCH THAT TECH
TO YOUR SCHOOL,
DISTRICT, OR EVENT!

Professional Development doesn't have to be a drag! When you hire Nate, Angie, and Matt to speak, you're giving your teachers, engaging, practical, and personalized training they can use the next day. Together, they've delivered keynotes, workshops, and conference sessions to thousands of teachers about technology and how to use it in the classroom.

Schedule Nate, Angie, and Matt to come speak to your school, staff, or students. We offer anything from short, one- to two-hour sessions to day-long trainings. Go to dontditchthattech.com/services to help us meet your needs!

Other Ways to Contact Nate & Angie:
Twitter: @teachfromridge
Instagram: @teachfromridge
Email: nate@teachingfromtheridge.com
Email: angie@teachingfromtheridge.com

Other Ways To Contact Matt:
Twitter: @jmattmiller
Email: matt@ditchthattextbook.com

ABOUT THE AUTHORS

MATT MILLER is a teacher, blogger and presenter from West Central Indiana. He has infused technology and innovative teaching methods in his classes for more than ten years. He is the author of the book *Ditch That Textbook: Free Your Teaching and Revolutionize Your Classroom* and *Ditch That Homework: Practical Strategies to Help Make Homework Obsolete.*

NATE RIDGWAY is a tech-loving history teacher in Indianapolis, Indiana. He specializes in lesson design and differentiation, and also is licensed in Special Education Mild Interventions. He has taught in both middle school and high school settings, and currently is enjoying teaching World History and Dual Credit U.S. History. He is finishing a master's degree in history at University of Indianapolis.

ANGIE RIDGWAY began her career in middle and high school teaching Spanish. She's now working with future secondary teachers and new faculty members at University of Indianapolis. Her passion lies in supporting new teachers' work in the implementation of original pedagogies that strive to meet all students' needs. She holds an ME and a PhD in curriculum and instruction with areas of emphasis in secondary education and Spanish.

CPSIA information can be obtained
at www.ICGtesting.com
Printed in the USA
BVHW051726100522
636644BV00006B/135